PETER GILL'S ROCK 'N' ROLL QUIZ BOOK

Peter Gill

Copyright © 2020 Peter Gill

All rights reserved.

ISBN: 9798576551729

DEDICATION

To those wonderful performers, songwriters and record producers that changed popular music forever.

CONTENTS

	Introduction	i
Quiz 1	Nice And Easy Does It	3
Quiz 2	The Birth Of Rock 'n' Roll	4
Quiz 3	Alan Freed	5
Quiz 4	Born To Rock 'n' Roll	6
Quiz 5	Chuck Berry	7
Quiz 6	Real Names	8
Quiz 7	Anagrams	9
Quiz 8	Bill Haley	10
Quiz 9	First Lines	11
Quiz 10	General Knowledge	12
Quiz 11	Eddie Cochran	13
Quiz 12	Skiffle	14
Quiz 13	Biopics	15
Quiz 14	Fats Domino	16
Quiz 15	Headlines	17
Quiz 16	Carl Perkins	18
Quiz 17	The Record Labels	19
Quiz 18	Buddy Holly	20
Quiz 19	The Songwriters	21
Quiz 20	General Knowledge 2	22

Quiz 21	Gene Vincent	23
Quiz 22	Where On Earth?	24
Quiz 23	Anagrams 2	25
Quiz 24	The Everly Brothers	26
Quiz 25	What's The Colour?	27
Quiz 26	The British Response	28
Quiz 27	Connie Francis	29
Quiz 28	Get A Job!	30
Quiz 29	Cliff Richard	31
Quiz 30	General Knowledge 3	32
Quiz 31	Album Titles	33
Quiz 32	Duane Eddy	34
Quiz 33	It's A Girl Thing!	35
Quiz 34	Little Richard	36
Quiz 35	In The Movies	37
Quiz 36	Billy Fury	38
Quiz 37	Anagrams 3	39
Quiz 38	Ricky Nelson	40
Quiz 39	On This Day	41
Quiz 40	General Knowledge 4	42
Quiz 41	Roy Orbison	43
Quiz 42	Name The Instrument	44
Quiz 43	Ray Charles	45

Quiz 44	Rock 'n' Roll Television	46
Quiz 45	Jerry Lee Lewis	47
Quiz 46	The Songwriters 2	48
Quiz 47	U.K. Number Ones	49
Quiz 48	The Groups	50
Quiz 49	Sam Phillips	51
Quiz 50	General Knowledge 5	52
Quiz 51	Anagrams 4	53
Quiz 52	Del Shannon	54
Quiz 53	Instrumentals	55
Quiz 54	Rock 'n' Roll Christmas	56
Quiz 55	Pat Boone	57
Quiz 56	Name The Year	58
Quiz 57	Wanda Jackson	59
Quiz 58	Name The Animal	60
Quiz 59	Whose Line Is It?	61
Quiz 60	General Knowledge 6	62
Quiz 61	Neil Sedaka	63
Quiz 62	Album Titles 2	64
Quiz 63	British Cover Versions	65
Quiz 64	Who Said That?	66
Quiz 65	It's A Boy Thing!	67
Quiz 66	Brenda Lee	68

Quiz 67	Anagrams 5	69
Quiz 68	It's All About The Nostalgia	70
Quiz 69	One Hit Wonders	71
Quiz 70	General Knowledge 7	72
Quiz 71	The Songwriters 3	73
Quiz 72	The Drifters	74
Quiz 73	Rock 'n' Roll Musicals	75
Quiz 74	Johnny Cash	76
Quiz 75	In The Movies 2	77
Quiz 76	What's The Number?	78
Quiz 77	Tommy Steele	79
Quiz 78	On This Day 2	80
Quiz 79	Sam Cooke	81
Quiz 80	General Knowledge 8	82
Quiz 81	U.S. Number Ones	83
Quiz 82	Bobby Vee	84
Quiz 83	Album Fillers	85
Quiz 84	Name The Instrument 2	86
Quiz 85	The Crickets	87
Quiz 86	The Live Albums	88
Quiz 87	Songs That Inspired The Film Title	89
Quiz 88	The Writers	90
Quiz 89	Shakin' Stevens	91

Quiz 90	General Knowledge 9	92
Quiz 91	First Lines 2	93
Quiz 92	Stars In Their Eyes	94
Quiz 93	The Stray Cats	95
Quiz 94	Whose Line Is It? 2	96
Quiz 95	'Covers' Albums	97
Quiz 96	The Songwriters 4	98
Quiz 97	Showaddywaddy	99
Quiz 98	Elvis	100
Quiz 99	Three Steps To Heaven	101
Quiz 100	It's Still Rock 'n' Roll To Me	102
	The Answers	103
	Further Listening	131

INTRODUCTION

Rock 'n' roll changed the world. It is a bold statement but it is 100% accurate. Without any doubt it was instrumental in the evolution of popular music, borne out by the numerous statements made by the generations of musicians that followed Elvis, Buddy, Chuck, Jerry Lee, Bill, Eddie, Gene et al that without them there wouldn't have been The Beatles, The Stones, The Who, Springsteen, Hendrix, Clapton, Bon Jovi and so many others.

But it wasn't just music that rock 'n' roll changed. It was a crucial ingredient in breaking down racial intolerances in the United States and at the centre was that greatest of catalyst, Elvis, a charismatic, good looking, young white boy that fused his love of country and gospel with blues and rhythm and blues to educate the white masses in the splendours of black rhythms. Elvis wasn't the first to sing rock 'n' roll, not by a long shot, but he was the one that took it and catapulted it into the stratosphere. Without rock 'n' roll and without Elvis the work of great social pioneers like Martin Luther King Jr would have been many times tougher.

And it empowered the youth. Bobby soxers had been recognised as an important economic consideration for a generation of marketing executives through the popularity of Bing Crosby and Frank Sinatra, but it was still the parents that held the purse strings. Rock 'n' roll gave the power to the teenagers, as they strived to fund their cravings for their idols it was their dollar, their pound that became an all-powerful influence in shifting the focus from the parents to the offspring. Music, clothing, magazines and films sought the teen market, the teen pennies and cents. The rise of teenagers, through the rise of rock 'n' roll, swayed opinions and influenced innovations. Teenagers held the power of success or failure, just as today the power is often with the microspends of the nine, ten and eleven year olds on games and music downloads.

This quiz book is meant as an homage to those to whom we owe so much. Rock 'n' roll as a musical form is not clearly defined by the very beauty of the fact that it is and always was a fusion of tastes and musical styles, but for the purpose of these questions, and my own passion, it deals with the music of the 1950s and early 1960s pre Beatlemania. Not that The Beatles weren't rock 'n' roll! Many would say, and I would be amongst them, that The Beatles were the greatest rock 'n' roll band to have walked the earth, but they were also so much more and were another catalyst that moved the world from its course. So, we have questions about the kings of rock 'n' roll, as there were many, not just one. Elvis, Jerry Lee, Buddy, Chuck, Eddie, Gene, Cliff, Connie, Wanda, Del, even Pat who it could be argued was as influential in his staid manner as Elvis in showing middle America the light. We have questions on the ones that came before, that were perhaps the real pioneers, that did the greatest work in shifting the beat and upping the tempo, the bluesmen and women, the country boys and girls and the rhythm and blues merchants. There are questions on the doo-wop groups, the teen idols that softened the edges of the genre then created 'pop', the country giants that started with rock 'n' roll then moved away. And there is a look at the revivalist musicians, those that had been brought up on the music and then kick-started a renewed interest when reaching their prime.

So, please enjoy these questions and tests, there may be some that you consider 'un rock 'n' roll' but I assure you they all have a link somewhere down the line. There will be artists, songs, albums and personalities that aren't represented – for these omissions I apologise - there is no intent.
What I hope is that this book reminds you of all the great music that has come and shall never be gone, so please, stick on some vinyl, put in a CD or ask Alexa to find a suitable playlist and commence, appreciate them all and …..

Hail! Hail! Rock 'n' Roll

Peter Gill – December 2020

THE QUESTIONS

QUIZ 1 - NICE AND EASY DOES IT

Some easy questions to get the ball rolling ……

1. Whose nickname was the Hillbilly Cat?

2. With which instrument is Jerry Lee Lewis most closely associated?

3. Who wrote *Johnny B Goode*?

4. With which band is Buddy Holly most closely associated?

5. What was disc jockey J.P. Richardson better known as?

6. In which city is Sun Recording Studios?

7. What is the title of the 1955 groundbreaking film starring Glenn Ford that caused riots, largely due to its inclusion of rock 'n' roll songs in its soundtrack?

8. Which rock 'n' roll legend almost lost his leg in a motorcycle accident in 1955 and walked with a pronounced limp for the rest of his life?

9. Which rock 'n' roll legend had hits with *Blueberry Hill*, *Ain't That A Shame*, *I'm Walkin'*, and *Walking To New Orleans* amongst others?

10. Which legendary rock 'n' roller released an album in 1962 entitled *The King of the Gospel Singers*?

QUIZ 2 – THE BIRTH OF ROCK 'N' ROLL

What the first rock 'n' roll record was or when it became a musical genre in its own right is impossible to delineate, but here are some questions on the theories and facts of the very earliest days:

1. Which Cleveland disc jockey is credited with coining the phrase rock 'n' roll?

2. A hugely popular and successful band leader from the 1930s to the 1950s who merged blues, jazz and boogie woogie, he is often referred to as the Grandfather of rock 'n' roll – who was he?

3. Released in 1939 what Big Joe Turner and Pete Johnson recording is a clear illustration of the evolution of popular music and sometimes suggested as the first rock 'n' roll record?

4. Who is the highly influential musician who was amongst the first to use heavy distortion on an electric guitar, has been referred to as the Godmother of rock 'n' roll and her 1944 recording of *Strange Things Happening Every Day* cited as the first rock 'n' roll record?

5. Written and recorded by Roy Brown in 1947 it is another strong contender for the first rock 'n' roll record, what is it?

6. In 1948 Roy Brown's song was covered by another pioneering musician and many have said that it is **his** version that is the first rock 'n' roll record, who is he?

7. *Rock Awhile* recorded by 18 year old guitarist and singer Goree Carter & His Hepcats and released on the Freedom Recording Company label has also been cited as the first rock 'n' roll record, when was it released?

8. Which Fats Domino record of 1949 is widely accepted as the first million selling rock 'n' roll record?

9. Others have suggested Elvis' first release on the Sun Records label in 1954 as the debut rock 'n' roll single, what was that recording?

10. However the most popularly accepted first rock 'n' roll record was made by Jackie Brenston and His Delta Cats and recorded by Sam Phillips on March 5 1951– what is it?

QUIZ 3 – ALAN FREED

He coined the phrase but what else do you know about Alan Freed? Try these questions to find out:

1. What name did Freed give to his WFW Cleveland radio show?

2. Known as the first rock 'n' roll concert, what was the show that Freed helped organise on March 21 1952?

3. In which film did Alan Freed state 'rock and roll is a river of music which has absorbed many streams: rhythm and blues, jazz, ragtime, cowboy songs, country songs, folk songs. All have contributed greatly to the big beat.'

4. What was the name of the radio show that Freed hosted when he moved to CBS in New York?

5. In which 1957 film, starring Freed, did performers LaVern Baker, Chuck Berry, Brook Benton, Frankie Lymon and world boxing champion Rocky Graziano all appear?

6. Why was Freed's primetime television series suddenly stopped after just four weeks?

7. Alan Freed is credited with co-writing several rock 'n' roll songs including Chuck Berry's *Maybellene* and The Moonglows' *Sincerely*. What did Harvey Fuqua of The Moonglows insist about Freed's contribution to *Sincerely*?

8. After a concert in Boston Freed was arrested for saying 'It looks like the Boston police don't want you to have a good time', with what was he charged?

9. What scandal brought a sudden and catastrophic end to Freed's career?

10. What age was Freed when he passed away of alcohol poisoning on January 20 1965?

QUIZ 4 – BORN TO ROCK 'N' ROLL

Which pioneering rock 'n' rollers were born on the following dates:

1. September 29 1935 in Ferriday, Louisiana (a piano pumper)

2. April 26 1938 in Corning, New York (he could twang)

3. October 3 1938 in Albert Lea, Minnesota (he got the blues in summer)

4. March 25 1933 in Bermondsey, London (you might have found him at the 2i's)

5. April 9 1932 in Tiptonville, Tennessee (don't step on his shoes)

6. October 20 1937 in Maud, Oklahoma (a rockabilly queen)

7. April 15 1939 in Blackheath, London (a bad boy)

8. December 11 1944 in Atlanta, Georgia (a small bundle of energy)

9. March 25 1934 in Memphis, Tennessee (a rockabilly boy)

10. April 23 1936 in Vernon, Texas (he drove all night)

QUIZ 5 – CHUCK BERRY

Ten questions on the man dubbed the Father of rock 'n' roll:

1. What was Chuck Berry's full name?

2. Why was Chuck sent to a reformatory in 1944?

3. Whose trio in St Louis, Missouri, did Chuck join in 1953?

4. Which blues legend suggested to Chuck that he ought to meet Leonard Chess of Chess Records?

5. Chuck's first release for Chess sold over a million copies, what was it?

6. The next of Chuck's singles to chart in the U.S. was *Roll Over Beethoven*, what was on the B side?

7. Released in 1957 what was the first album that Chuck released called?

8. What was the first single of Chuck's to chart in the U.K.?

9. What recording of Chuck's features in Quentin Tarantino's film *Pulp Fiction* when John Travolta and Uma Thurman enter a twist competition?

10. What was the only single to top the U.K. charts for Chuck when it did so for four weeks in 1972?

QUIZ 6 – REAL NAMES

Give the better known names of the following:

1. Richard Penniman

2. Ronald Wycherley

3. Vincent Eugene Craddock

4. Harry Webb

5. Reginald Smith

6. Thomas Hicks

7. Charles Hardin Holley

8. Ernest Evans

9. Concetta Franconero

10. David Spencer

QUIZ 7 – ANAGRAMS

Decipher these rock 'n' roll artists:

1. Rainy folk men

2. Silvery sleep

3. Honky dj din

4. Minds afoot

5. My omelettes

6. Rhino acceded

7. Hustling camcorders

8. Jackdaws anon

9. Joint buerger

10. Avenge Eric

QUIZ 8 - BILL HALEY

Questions on the man with the famous kiss curl:

1. Where was Bill Haley born?

2. With what disability did Bill Haley live from the age of four?

3. During the 1940s Haley was particularly famed for a style of country singing, what was it?

4. Released in April 1953, what record of Bill Haley with Haley's Comets is marked as the first of the rock 'n' roll genre to appear on the American music charts?

5. Following the success of that record what was the band's name changed to?

6. Which of his recordings, in December 1954, became the first rock 'n' roll song to enter the British charts?

7. What was the name of the 1958 album that included such titles as *Mo Rock-a-Hula*, *Piccadilly Rock*, *Rockin Rollin Schnitzelbank* and *Rockin Matilda*?

8. What was the B side to the 1956 release *R-O-C-K*?

9. Featured in the 1956 film *Rock Around The Clock* who was *Rudy's Rock* titled after?

10. Aged just 55, what was the official cause given for Bill's death in 1981?

QUIZ 9 – FIRST LINES

What songs are these the first lines to:

1. You know I can be found sitting home all alone

2. Oh well I'm the type of guy who will never settle down

3. I feel so bad I've got a worried mind

4. Deep down in Louisiana close to New Orleans

5. In a little café just the other side of the border

6. It was a moonlight night in old Mexico

7. Gonna tell Aunt Mary 'bout Uncle John

8. If you hear somebody knocking on your door

9. Get outta that bed, wash your face and hands

10. Each time we have a quarrel it almost breaks my heart

QUIZ 10 - GENERAL KNOWLEDGE

Some questions to test your all round rock 'n' roll knowledge:

1. What was the nickname of Alan Freed?

2. Which historic recording studio will you still find at 706 Union Avenue, Memphis, Tennessee?

3. What is the name of the song that was a 1958 hit for The Olympics on the Demon record label?

4. *It's All In The Game* was a number 2 hit for Cliff Richard in 1963 but who had the original 1958 hit with it?

5. How is Harold Lloyd Jenkins better known?

6. How many U.K. top ten hits did Jerry Lee Lewis have?

7. How did Johnny Burnette die?

8. What was the number one hit song for actor Tab Hunter in 1957?

9. Which British popular artist played the piano on Gene Vincent's recording of *Pistol Packin' Mama*?

10. In the 1978 nostalgia musical *Grease* who makes an appearance as Teen Angel?

QUIZ 11 - EDDIE COCHRAN

Ten teasers on the superb Eddie Cochran:

1. Early in his musical career Eddie performed with Hank Cochran as 'The Cochran Brothers', but what actual relation to Eddie was Hank?

2. In July 1956 Eddie released his first record as a solo performer, on which record label was it released?

3. That first solo single had the song *Half Loved* on the flip side, but what was on the A side?

4. In 1957 Eddie appeared in his second film (the first being *The Girl Can't Help It*), starring Mamie Van Doren and Lori Nelson, what was it called?

5. On which record label did Eddie release his only album during his lifetime in 1957?

6. With whom did Eddie collaborate to write *Summertime Blues*?

7. What was Eddie's follow up single to *Summertime Blues*?

8. Written by disc jockey Tommy Dee, what song did Eddie record in tribute to Buddy Holly, Ritchie Valens and The Big Bopper after their tragic death?

9. Eddie's fiancée at the time of his death was Sharon Sheeley who was also in the car crash that would cause his death. What song, her first, was Ricky Nelson's first US number one?

10. Eddie's only UK number 1 was *Three Steps To Heaven* released in the UK in May 1960, but who performed on drums and lead guitar respectively on the record?

QUIZ 12 - SKIFFLE

Skiffle was a precursor to rock 'n' roll whose revival in the U.K. in the 1950s nurtured many rock 'n' roll performers, what do you know about it?

1. In the U.K. who was the recognized King of Skiffle?

2. A number 8 hit in both the U.K. and U.S. what was the King of Skiffle's debut release?

3. With which song did Chas McDevitt and his skiffle group have a number 5 hit featuring Nancy Whiskey?

4. A Liverpudlian teenage skiffle group of the 1950s, who would The Quarrymen gradually morph into?

5. Which group, that included Wally Whyton, had a number 10 hit on the U.K. charts in 1957 with *Don't You Rock Me Daddy-O*?

6. American skiffle and bluegrass musician Johnny Duncan had a number 2 hit in the U.K. in 1957 with which song?

7. Which BBC television programme that was launched in 1957 helped to popularise both skiffle and rock 'n' roll?

8. Which skiffle group performed the theme song of this BBC television programme?

9. Which coffee bar, found at 59 Old Compton Street, Soho, London played a formative role in the emergence of both skiffle and rock 'n' roll in the U.K.?

10. What was the name of the skiffle and rock 'n' roll group that was formed by Barry Gibb in Manchester in 1955 that eventually became the Bee Gees?

QUIZ 13 - BIOPICS

Which icons were the following biopics about:

1. *Walk The Line*

2. *La Bamba*

3. *Telstar*

4. *Cadillac Records*

5. *Backbeat*

6. *Beyond The Sea*

7. *What's Love Got To Do With It*

8. *Jersey Boys*

9. *Deadman's Curve*

10. *American Hot Wax*

QUIZ 14 - FATS DOMINO

Some questions on the wonderful Fats Domino:

1. In which city was Fats born?

2. What is Fats' real name?

3. With whom did Fats collaborate in writing over forty hits including *I Hear You Knocking*, *Ain't That A Shame*, *Blue Monday* and *I'm Walkin*?

4. With which record company did Fats sign a contract in 1949?

5. On which influential and much covered 1952 Lloyd Price recording did Fats add his rolling piano style?

6. What song was on the B side to Fats' 1955 release *Ain't That A Shame*?

7. Of Fats' many hits, *Blueberry Hill* is perhaps his most famous - what was the highest chart position that it reached in the U.K.?

8. Released in March 1956 what was Fats' debut album entitled?

9. In which 1980 released Clint Eastwood film did Fats make a cameo appearance performing *Whiskey Heaven*?

10. In which natural disaster of August 2005 was Fats feared killed before being rescued by the Coast Guard?

QUIZ 15 - HEADLINES

For whom were the following headlines written:

1. Along Comes A New Contender For The 'King Of Din' Title – New Musical Express 1956

2. 'Don't Call Me Another Presley …. I'm Just A Happy Singer' Says New R & R Star – Record Mirror October 1956

3. 'He's Never Made A Record That Wasn't A Hit!' – New Musical Express September 1957

4. 'I Always Wanted To be A Comedian But … I'm A Hit Singer Instead!' – New Musical Express November 1957

5. Will The Army Harm His Career? – New Musical Express January 1958

6. From Timber Yard To Television – Disc March 1958

7. Police Check Up On Child Bride – Daily Mirror May 1958

8. Top 'Rock' Stars Die In Crash – Daily Mirror February 4 1959

9. Crash Kills Boy Rock Star – Daily Sketch April 18 1960

10. 'Girls Who Gave Lads 'Quivers Down The Membranes' Inspired My Hit' – New Musical Express 1960

QUIZ 16 - CARL PERKINS

Some questions on that early exponent of rockabilly to get your head round:

1. What were the names of Carl's two brothers who performed with him in the early 1950s?

2. Upon which record label was Carl's debut single *Movie Magg* released?

3. Which song written and recorded by Carl would be the first million seller for a Sun Records artist?

4. Carl was involved in a serious car accident in March 1956 in which he nearly died and in which his brother Jay sustained injuries that would ultimately lead to his early death. To whose television show in New York was Carl travelling at the time of the accident?

5. Carl's first album included *Honey Don't*, *Your True Love* and *Boppin' The Blues* - what was it titled?

6. With which other past Sun recording artist did Carl tour with for ten years as part of his revue?

7. What song did Carl write in 1968 which went to the top of the U.S. country charts for Johnny Cash?

8. Which two Perkins' songs did the Beatles record for their album *Beatles For Sale*?

9. Which British blues band performed *Matchbox* with Carl live on the Johnny Cash Show in 1969?

10. With whom did Carl collaborate in 1981 on the song *Get It* which appeared on the chart topping album *Tug Of War*?

QUIZ 17 – THE RECORD LABELS

Identify the record labels that released the following classic recordings in their country of recording:

1. Fats Domino's *Blueberry Hill*

2. Bill Haley and his Comets' *Rock Around The Clock*

3. The Crickets' *That'll Be The Day*

4. Ray Charles' *What'd I Say*

5. Johnny Kidd and the Pirates' *Shakin' All Over*

6. Eddie Cochran's *C'mon Everybody*

7. Gene Vincent's *Bluejean Bop!*

8. Little Richard's *Good Golly Miss Molly*

9. Frankie Lymon & the Teenagers' *Why Do Fools Fall In Love*

10. The Platters' *The Great Pretender*

QUIZ 18 - BUDDY HOLLY

A selection of questions on the legendary Buddy Holly:

1. Where was Buddy born?

2. With whom did Buddy perform as the duo 'Buddy and Bob'?

3. With which record company did Buddy have his first recording contract?

4. In April 1956 Buddy's first record was released. *Blue Days, Black Nights* was on the A side, what was on the B side?

5. What was the name of the studio owner and subsequent manager of the Crickets who would go on to record most of Buddy's biggest hits?

6. Which film had Buddy and Jerry Allison seen that inspired them to write *That'll Be The Day*?

7. Buddy's releases would variously be under his own name or that of the Crickets largely due to contractual reasons, under what name was *Oh Boy* released?

8. What is perhaps unusual about the cover photograph of Buddy for his eponymous debut studio album released on February 20 1958?

9. Who did Buddy marry on August 15 1958?

10. What was Buddy's first posthumous hit single?

QUIZ 19 – THE SONGWRITERS

Who is credited with penning the following songs:

1. *Hound Dog*

2. *Bye Bye Love*

3. *Living Doll*

4. *Breathless*

5. *Summertime Blues*

6. *That'll Be The Day*

7. *Singing The Blues*

8. *Under The Moon Of Love*

9. *Blueberry Hill*

10. *Oh, Pretty Woman*

QUIZ 20 - GENERAL KNOWLEDGE 2

Some more questions to test your general rock 'n' roll knowledge:

1. Which Coasters' song written by Leiber and Stoller did Elvis perform in his 1964 movie *Roustabout*?

2. Which British rocker had a number 3 hit in 1960 with the Fats Waller standard *Ain't Misbehavin'*?

3. What was the name of the duo who, in 1957 would have a minor hit with their heavily Everly Brothers influenced song *Hey Schoolgirl*?

4. Which girl group had a 1958 hit both sides of the Atlantic with *Born Too Late*?

5. With which Ritchie Valens song did Tommy Steele have a U.K. hit in 1958?

6. On which record label did Ruth Brown release her 1957 compilation album *Rock & Roll*?

7. How did singer Johnny Ace die?

8. With which Big Joe Turner song, released in July 1956, did Shakin' Stevens have a number 11 hit in the U.K. in 1985?

9. What is the name of the pioneering disc jockey on Memphis' WHBQ radio station that debuted many of rock 'n' roll's brightest stars and their releases?

10. What is the date which Don McLean says the music died?

QUIZ 21 - GENE VINCENT

Ten questions on the fabulous Gene Vincent:

1. What was the name of Gene Vincent's band?

2. And why were they so named?

3. With which record company did Gene sign a recording contract in 1956?

4. *Be Bop A Lula* is the song he will always be associated most with but originally it was chosen as a B side to what song?

5. What was the follow up single to the success of *Be Bop A Lula*?

6. Who was the influential guitarist of the Blue Caps on 35 of Gene's recordings including *Be Bop A Lula*, *Race With The Devil*, *Cat Man*, *Bluejean Bop* and *Double Talkin' Baby*?

7. In which film did Gene make an appearance performing *Be Bop A Lula* in a rehearsal studio?

8. Which British television producer has been credited with changing Gene's image when he appeared on his television show *Boy Meets Girl* in black leathers and wearing an ostentatious gold medallion?

9. With which other legendary rock 'n' roller was Gene touring Britain in April 1960 when he was involved in a serious motor accident?

10. Gene was just 36 when he died. What was the cause of his death?

QUIZ 22 - WHERE ON EARTH?

From these clues identify the town, city or country:

1. Where did Chuck Berry's Greyhound bus break down and leave them all stranded?

2. Where did Jerry Lee Lewis say was the land of dreams?

3. Where did Wilbert Harrison say there was a crazy way of lovin'?

4. Where did Elvis say there lived a girl that even made the alligators look tame?

5. Where were Johnny Cash and June Carter heading after getting married in a fever?

6. Where did the Everly Brothers say was the dearest land outside Heaven to them?

7. Working all day without the sun shining, where did Roy Orbison dream of getting back to?

8. After Macon, Georgia where did Jerry Reed thumb his way down to?

9. Where did Little Richard want to return where the magnolia smells sweet and the white cotton is warm?

10. Where did The Drifters say the neon lights were bright?

QUIZ 23 - ANAGRAMS 2

Decipher these anagrams to find ten classic rock 'n' roll songs:

1. Technical Ally

2. eBay Bamby

3. Starlet

4. Yukon Scout

5. Damn Betsy

6. Trite tepee

7. Taiwan Moog

8. Albert Hess

9. Denny Otho

10. Thy loony Ellen

QUIZ 24 - THE EVERLY BROTHERS

Ten questions on those golden voiced boys, Phil and Don:

1. Which was the older brother?

2. When appearing on their father's radio show as children, how were the brothers introduced?

3. What song became their first million seller?

4. What was the follow-up hit to their first million seller, both for the brothers and the songwriters, that reached number one in the U.S. charts and number two in the U.K.?

5. *All I Have To Dream* was the brothers' first U.K. number one, what was their second?

6. Their 1960 hit *Let It Be Me* is based on which French song?

7. What did the brothers do in October 1961 which saw them immediately drop out of the spotlight?

8. On July 14 1973 the brothers broke up in spectacular fashion, where did it happen?

9. Released in March 1977 what was the name of Don's third solo album release?

10. Where was their reunion concert staged on September 23 1983?

QUIZ 25 – WHAT'S THE COLOUR?

Find the colour from these clues :

1. Doc Pomus and Mort Shuman song that Elvis recorded in 1960 and released as the B side to *It's Now Or Never*.

2. Originally a hit in the States for Jim Lowe in 1956, Frankie Vaughan had a number two hit in the U.K. with it, then Shakin' Stevens took it to the top of the charts in 1981.

3. Nothing to do with the Peanuts comic strip, this was a Leiber and Stoller hit for The Coasters in 1959.

4. The flowers that Bobby Darin wrote and sang about in 1963.

5. The 1961 A side to *Walk Right Back* for the Everly Brothers.

6. Johnny Cash recorded song and his 21st released album in 1965.

7. 1958 song written and recorded by Carl Perkins on Sun Records that was covered by Jerry Lee Lewis but not Elvis.

8. One eyed, one horned and it flew, and it was a hit for Sheb Wooley in 1958.

9. These sails would give Fats Domino his last hit in his lifetime when it reached 35 in 1963.

10. Great instrumental from 1963 by Jet Harris and Tony Meehan.

QUIZ 26 – THE BRITISH RESPONSE

Rock 'n' roll soon crossed the Atlantic, can you answer these questions on the British response?

1. What Ritchie Valens songs did Marty Wilde take to number 3 in the U.K. charts in 1959?

2. With what song did Eden Kane have a number 1 hit in 1961?

3. Tommy Steele had a number 13 hit in the U.K. charts in 1956 with what debut single?

4. Which diminutive energetic rocker released the self-penned *Rockin at the 2 T's* on the Decca label in 1958?

5. What was the first song to give Adam Faith a number 1 hit in the U.K.?

6. Latterly an eccentric political party leader, what 1963 release is the song most associated with the charismatic Screaming Lord Sutch?

7. Mike Berry and the Outlaws had a string of releases produced by Joe Meek, his first hit on the U.K. charts which reached number 24, was banned by the B.B.C.. What was it and why was it banned?

8. Billy Fury's second single release and a number 28 hit in the U.K. was *Margo*, but what great track was on the B side?

9. An absolute classic, which is the song written and recorded by Johnny Kidd that gave him, with his Pirates, a number 1 hit in August 1960?

10. Cliff Richard's third single release and a number 20 hit in the U.K. had a very similar title to the single that would be his fifth release and a number 1 hit. What was that third single called?

QUIZ 27 – CONNIE FRANCIS

One of the highest selling artists of the 1950s and 1960s, try these questions on the lovely Connie Francis:

1. For whom did Connie dub the vocals in the 1957 film that also starred Paul Carr and featured Frankie Avalon, Buddy Knox and Carl Perkins?

2. After several attempts, her first chart success was the single *The Majesty Of Love* in 1957 - with whom did she duet on the single?

3. Her next release gave her a number 4 hit in the U.S. and a number 1 in the U.K. - what was it?

4. What Howard Greenfield and Neil Sedaka composition gave Connie her second U.K. number 1?

5. In 1958 she would be required to dub the singing voice in a film for the third time, this time it was for the British film *The Sheriff of Fractured Jaw* - whose voice did she dub?

6. In 1959 she had a double sided hit single both sides of the Atlantic, *Frankie* was on the B side - what was on the A side?

7. In 1960 Connie got to actually star in a film, and also had a hit with the title song - what was the name of the film and song?

8. In 1959 Connie released her first album singing in a foreign language, something that she would repeat several times through her career - what was that first album called?

9. In 1962 Connie had her final top ten hit in the U.K. and U.S. - what great release was that hit?

10. With which flamboyant pianist did Connie appear in her 1965 film *When The Boys Meet The Girls*?

QUIZ 28 - GET A JOB!

Try these questions on the other jobs that some rock 'n' rollers did before, during or after their music careers:

1. Which rock 'n' roller, after leaving the army returned to Michigan to sell carpets and drive a truck for a furniture factory before making it big as a musician?

2. Which legendary rock 'n' roller, for a period during the height of his music success, had a career change to tour the United States as an evangelist preacher?

3. Who was a child radio and television star before becoming one of the top selling rock 'n' roll artists of the 50s and 60s?

4. Which piano pumping wildman once tried to sell vacuum cleaners for a living?

5. Which Welsh singer once worked as an upholsterer and milkman before finding success in the West End as Elvis?

6. Which crossover star served in the US Air Force as a morse code operator?

7. Which singer and songwriter from Louisiana went on to manage Icon Food Brands which specialise in Southern-style foods such as Lawdy Miss Clawdy food products?

8. Which highly influential performer, after leaving school, became a cook and bartender, then becoming known as 'The Singing Barman' performed with boogie woogie pianist Pete Johnson?

9. Which British rock 'n' roller worked on a tugboat and as a docker before he was to find stardom?

10. Who worked as a painter and decorator and also a janitor before finding recording success?

QUIZ 29 – CLIFF RICHARD

Some questions on one of the finest rock 'n' rollers to emerge from the U.K.:

1. Cliff Richard is the third bestselling artist in U.K. singles chart history, who is he behind?

2. In what country was Cliff Richard born?

3. What was the name of the group that he fronted which would gradually morph into The Shadows?

4. What is the title of Cliff's first release that is largely regarded as the U.K.'s first authentic rock 'n' roll record?

5. What was Cliff's first U.K. number 1, which due to its popularity in the U.S. forced his backing band to change their name to The Shadows?

6. In 1962 Cliff had a number two U.K. hit with Jack Clement's *It'll Be Me*. Who originally recorded the song in 1957?

7. In which 1963 film does Cliff and his friends decide to take a London bus across continental Europe?

8. Which 1976 single reached number 6 in the U.S. Billboard Hot 100, his highest position in the States?

9. With which rock 'n' roll legend did Cliff collaborate for the 1983 released single *She Means Nothing To Me*?

10. Released on November 11 2013 what is the name of the album that was promoted as Cliff's 100th?

QUIZ 30 – GENERAL KNOWLEDGE 3

Some more questions to test your general rock 'n' roll knowledge:

1. Who had a number one hit in the States in 1956 with *Rock and Roll Waltz*?

2. Which 1958 number 1 hit in the States for David Seville saved Liberty Records from near-bankruptcy?

3. *Brand New Cadillac* is regarded as a classic British rock 'n' roll song, who wrote and recorded it?

4. What is the real name of British rocker Vince Eager?

5. Which British multi-instrumentalist recorded with Jerry Lee Lewis, Bill Haley, Gene Vincent, Cliff Bennett, Mike Berry and many, many others but is best known for co-creating the music style 'Rockney' with Dave Peacock?

6. Featuring on most of Little Richard's and Fats Domino's hits, with what instrument is rock 'n' roll pioneer Earl Palmer associated?

7. Who had a number 52 hit in the States in 1957 with his recording of his own song *Rockin' Pneumonia and the Boogie Woogie Flu*?

8. With whom did Jerry Butler have a number 11 hit in the States in 1958 with the song *For Your Precious Love*?

9. Shirley Goodman and Leonard Lee wrote and recorded their 1956 hit with which they had a number 20 in the U.S. - what was the song called and under what name did they release it?

10. With which song did John Leyton go to the top of the British charts on August 9 1961?

QUIZ 31 – ALBUM TITLES

So many albums have eponymous titles or name the artists, but who released these?

1. *Let The Four Winds Blow* (1961)

2. *The Greatest Live Show On Earth* (1964)

3. *Handy Man* (1964)

4. *Good Rockin' Then and Now* (1974)

5. *Songs Our Daddy Taught Us* (1958)

6. *Sings ….. Guess Who?* (1963)

7. *Muscle Beach Party And Other Motion Picture Songs* (1963)

8. *After School Session* (1957)

9. *Singin' To My Baby* (1957)

10. *He's So Fine* (1958)

QUIZ 32 – DUANE EDDY

Try these questions on the master guitarist:

1. Who was the former disc jockey that would produce many of Duane's hits and himself have a notable solo career and collaboration with Nancy Sinatra?

2. What was Duane's breakthrough hit that gave him a number 6 hit in the States and number 19 in the U.K.?

3. Duane's next three releases *Ramrod, Cannonball* and *The Lonely One* all featured on his debut album, what was it called?

4. On what record label were Duane's singles released in the U.K. until late 1961?

5. Duane had two number 2 hits in the U.K., what were they?

6. On the cover of Duane's 1961 album *Girls! Girls! Girls!* Eddy appears with which female diminutive rock 'n' roller?

7. On Duane's 1962 hit *Dance With The Guitar Man* which female group provided the vocals?

8. Duane appeared in a few films - what was the 1961 western that starred Richard Boone, George Hamilton, Luana Patten and Arthur O'Connell and also featured Charles Bronson, Richard Chamberlain and Slim Pickens?

9. Who did Duane collaborate with on a reworking of his 1959 hit *Peter Gunn*?

10. What was Duane's favoured guitar?

QUIZ 33 – IT'S A GIRL THING!

What is the girl's name in the following songs:

1. In 1961 Elvis sang about her being 'his latest flame'

2. According to Little Richard she was built sweet and gave Uncle John everything he needed

3. The Everly Brothers begged her to wake up

4. Roy Orbison told his mama and dad that she was the sweetest little girl in the whole world

5. Larry Williams said that she made him dizzy

6. Paul Anka was so young and she was so old

7. Who Buster Brown sang about in his 1960 minor hit on the U.S. charts

8. A 1962 Four Seasons chart topper in the U.S. and number 8 in the U.K.

9. According to Buddy Holly she got married

10. Tommy Roe's 1962 U.S. chart topper and U.K. number 3

QUIZ 34 – LITTLE RICHARD

Test your knowledge on one of rock 'n' roll's most flamboyant performers:

1. Where was Little Richard born on December 5 1932?

2. For whom did Richard record his first four singles, before being released from his contract?

3. What was the stage name of the flamboyant artist that influenced Richard's performances, style and supposedly taught him to play the piano?

4. What is the song that Richard co-wrote with Dorothy LaBostrie that was released in October 1955 and cemented his status in popular music history?

5. His follow up single was *Long Tall Sally* but what classic song was on the B side?

6. What was the name of the backing band that Richard put together following his recording successes?

7. Released in 1957 what was the title of Richard's debut album?

8. Which legendary guitarist joined Richard's band in the tail end of 1964 but would leave the following summer complaining of being owed money?

9. What was the title of the album released in 1971 for Reprise records that made a bold claim that only he and a very small number of others could possibly claim?

10. With whom did Richard sing a duet on the song *You Really Got Me Now* as part of the soundtrack to the film *Young Guns*?

QUIZ 35 – IN THE MOVIES

Answer these questions on rock 'n' roll stars on the big screen:

1. Which 1956 film starring Jayne Mansfield and Tom Ewell had appearances by Little Richard, Fats Domino and Eddie Cochran?

2. Which Elvis Presley film was based on the Harold Robbins' novel *A Stone For Danny Fisher*?

3. In which film featuring Alan Freed was Tuesday Weld's singing voice dubbed by Connie Francis?

4. Which 1958 film's opening scene sees Jerry Lee Lewis perform the title song?

5. In which film did Ritchie Valens make his one and only cameo appearance?

6. What was the first feature film that Cliff Richard appeared in?

7. What is the name of the Tommy Steele movie vehicle that saw him play the two roles of Tony Whitecliffe and Tommy Hudson?

8. In which film did Alan Dale star as Arnie Haines and Little Richard performed Tutti Frutti and Long Tall Sally?

9. What film saw Bill Haley and his Comets perform *See You Later Alligator*, *Rock-A-Beatin Boogie* and the title track?

10. Which 1962 film starred Billy Fury as Billy Universe and also featured Helen Shapiro and Bobby Vee?

QUIZ 36 – BILLY FURY

Some questions on one of the finest rock 'n' rollers to emerge from the U.K.:

1. Where was Billy Fury born?

2. Who was the famous manager and impresario that promoted him and pushed Billy to change his name?

3. Billy's first single was *Maybe Tomorrow* on the Decca label, what was on the B side?

4. Billy's first album, released in 1960, is highly regarded, both for the quality of its content and that all the songs were penned by Billy, what is it called?

5. John Lennon turned down the chance for his band to become Billy's backing band. What was the name of John's band at that time?

6. Released in 1965 what is the name of the second feature film starring Billy?

7. Which massive hit for Billy in 1960 reignited interest in him when it was used over forty years later to advertise Toyota Yaris cars on U.K. television?

8. Which Elvis song featured in the film *Girls! Girls! Girls!* did Billy cover and release as a single in 1962 and on his album *Best Of Billy Fury*?

9. What was the name of Billy's character in the 1973 film *That'll Be The Day*?

10. Billy died on January 28 1983 aged 42, he had had a weak heart for much of his life from contracting what as a child?

QUIZ 37 – ANAGRAMS 3

Decipher these rock 'n' roll groups:

1. Shortest AEC

2. Desert Firth

3. Health cents

4. ABC dominates hellishly

5. Alf Something

6. Kitsch Crete

7. Hometown logs

8. Chevrolets

9. Hatter slept

10. Demonise Hot

QUIZ 38 – RICKY NELSON

One of the most successful recording stars of all time, can you answer these questions on Rick(y) Nelson:

1. What was Ricky's real name?

2. In which U.S. State was Ricky born on May 8 1940?

3. What was the name of the radio and television series that Ricky starred in from the age of eight?

4. Which Fats Domino song appeared on Ricky's first single?

5. Ricky's first hit in the U.K. was his first single of 1958, what was it?

6. Who was the eighteen year old lead guitarist that Ricky signed to his band in time to record *Believe What You Say* who would later be Elvis' first call guitarist from 1969 to his death?

7. With which double A single did Ricky have his highest charting U.K. hit?

8. What was the name of the backing band that (now known as) Rick formed in 1969 that appeared on the *Rick Sings Nelson* album?

9. His last significant charting single came in 1972 and reached number 6 in the U.S., what was it and what inspired it?

10. From whom had Ricky Nelson bought the Douglas DC-3 aircraft in which he was killed on New Year's Eve 1985?

QUIZ 39 – ON THIS DAY

Important dates in rock 'n' roll music history, try these questions:

1. December 1 1957 – which two acts performed on the Ed Sullivan Show?

2. October 11 1955 – which three Sun Records artists commenced an eleven date tour of southern U.S. states?

3. May 15 1961 – which Nashville based piano player topped the U.K. singles chart?

4. February 3 1967 – which British record producer shot his landlady and then himself at his London flat?

5. October 8 2020 – which former bass player of British groups The Wildcats and The Shadows passed away at the age of 81?

6. December 12 1937 – which female recording sensation was born in New Jersey?

7. September 19 1957 – which 16 year old joined the Dick Teague Skiffle Group?

8. October 16 1951 – which 18 year old made his first recordings for R.C.A. in Atlanta?

9. June 13 1972 – which former singer of The Drifters died of a heart attack in New York?

10. December 10 1949 – who recorded his first tracks for Imperial Records?

QUIZ 40 – GENERAL KNOWLEDGE 4

Yet more questions to test your general rock 'n' roll knowledge:

1. Who said 'If you had to give rock 'n' roll another name, you might call it Chuck Berry'?

2. Which 50s legend is generally considered the King of Rockabilly?

3. In what 1963 film did Marty Wilde and Joe Brown have starring roles and Freddie and the Dreamers make an appearance?

4. As of Christmas 2020 what is the last Eddie Cochran song to chart in the U.K.?

5. Recorded and made a hit by numerous artists, who recorded *Route 66* first?

6. Whose memoirs were entitled *My Life, Through The Eye of a Tornado*?

7. During 1958 and 1959 Elvis placed eleven hits on the U.S. Hot 100, how many did Ricky Nelson place in the same period?

8. Who did Bobby Darin famously marry on December 1 1960?

9. In 1966 The Ventures had a minor hit with an instrumental version of the title song of a famous television series of the period. What was the song, and from which series did it come?

10. Which Buddy Holly B side gave The Rolling Stones their first top ten U.K. hit?

QUIZ 41 – ROY ORBISON

One of the true rock 'n' roll songwriting pioneers with an astonishing voice, Roy would be one of the most successful recording artists of the 60s, how much do you know about him?

1. With which group did Roy Orbison get his first recording contract with Sam Phillips and release his first single?

2. Roy's second release had a self-penned B side, what was that song?

3. What was the title of Roy's first album, released on the Sun record label?

4. What Orbison song did the Everly Brothers record and release as the B side to *All I Have To Do Is Dream*?

5. With which record label would Roy find his greatest success on the U.S. charts?

6. A number 2 hit in the U.S. and a number 1 in the U.K. in 1960 what was the song that gave Roy his first real taste of stardom?

7. With which song did Roy have his first number 1 hit in the U.S.?

8. In 1964 Roy would have successive number 1 hits in the U.K., the second of which was *Oh, Pretty Woman*, what was the first?

9. As one of the Travelling Wilburys Roy gave himself the name Lefty Wilbury, what was the inspiration from which he took his name?

10. What was the name of the posthumous album released just two months after Roy's passing?

QUIZ 42 – NAME THE INSTRUMENT

With which instrument would you identify the following maestros:

1. James Burton

2. Johnnie Johnson

3. King Curtis (Curtis Ousley)

4. Little Walter

5. Joe B Mauldin

6. D J Fontana

7. Franny (Francis) Beecher

8. Boots Randolph (Homer Louis Randolph III)

9. Floyd Cramer

10. Kenny Lovelace

QUIZ 43 – RAY CHARLES

A ground breaking artist who fused so many music genres both in his performances and compositions that to many he was known as the Genius. What do you know about him?

1. Who is quoted as saying that Ray was 'the only true genius in show business'?

2. How did Ray lose his eyesight?

3. Which fellow pianist and singer was a strong influence on Ray during his early career, which his first recordings bear witness to?

4. On which record label did Ray release the 1953 single *Mess Around*?

5. In 1954 he would have another hit on the U.S. R&B charts, this time with a song written by Memphis Curtis, what was it?

6. His first number 1 hit (again on the R&B charts) was self-penned and released in 1954, what was it?

7. Released in 1959 what was Ray's first U.S. nationally charting album called?

8. What was the name of the female backing group that added their vocals to many of Ray's recordings?

9. A number 1 hit in the U.S., what was the only recording of Ray's to also top the charts in the U.K.?

10. In which 1980s film did Ray make a cameo appearance performing *Shake A Tailfeather*?

QUIZ 44 – ROCK 'N' ROLL TELEVISION

There have been a number of television shows and specials that have immortalised rock 'n' roll, answer these questions on some of them:

1. Hosted by Alan Freed, what was the first prime time rock 'n' roll dance show on U.S. television that debuted on May 4 1957?

2. Elvis' television special of 1968 for NBC is known as his Comeback Special, however it was originally advertised as being presented by its main sponsor. What was that sponsor?

3. Broadcast in 1988 what was the title of the Roy Orbison television special that included such guests as Bruce Springsteen, Tom Waits, Elvis Costello and Bonnie Raitt?

4. Filmed at the Storyville nightclub in New Orleans, which legendary piano players appeared with Fats Domino in the live special *Fats and Friends*?

5. Filmed in the late 1980s, from where did Wolfman Jack present his live rock 'n' roll television shows which included such artists as Del Shannon and The Shirelles?

6. Whose TV Special of 1982 to celebrate 25 years in music included performances by Johnny Cash, Kris Kristofferson, Mickey Gilley, Carl Perkins and Charlie Rich?

7. Filmed in 2001 in Pittsburgh what was the live tv special called that included performances from Little Richard, Frankie Valli, Lloyd Price, The Five Satins, The Imperials and many others?

8. In 1985 George Harrison, Eric Clapton, Dave Edmunds, Ringo Starr and others appeared with Carl Perkins for a television special. What was the title of the show?

9. Airing on British television in 1958 and 1959 what was the name of Jack Good's all-music teenage show on ITV?

10. Who was the host of the 1984 television special called *Super Night of Rock 'n' Roll* which featured vintage film and live performances from Chuck Berry, James Brown, Bob Gaudio, Darlene Love, Ronnie Spector and Martha Reeves amongst many others?

QUIZ 45 – JERRY LEE LEWIS

Test your knowledge on the first wildman of rock 'n' roll:

1. Since his childhood Jerry has been known by his nickname, what is it?

2. What was the first song recorded and released by Jerry on Sun Records?

3. What was the title of the second outstanding single he released that would see him top the U.S. country and R&B charts and reach number 3 on the Hot 100 and number 8 in the U.K.?

4. In which 1957 film did Jerry perform his most famous hit *Great Balls of Fire*?

5. Apart from her being only thirteen at the time and a first cousin once removed, why else was Jerry Lee's third marriage to Myra Brown scandalous?

6. Which Jerry Lee Lewis album from 1964 is widely recognised as one of the greatest live rock 'n' roll albums ever?

7. Jerry, whilst at Sun Records, often acted as a session musician on other artists' records. Who recorded *Flyin' Saucers Rock and Roll* that had Jerry on piano?

8. In 1986 *The Class of '55* album was released. Who were the other members of that class?

9. In 1961 with which Ray Charles classic did Jerry have a number ten hit in the U.K. charts?

10. Who wrote the 2014 biography *Jerry Lee Lewis: His Own Story*?

QUIZ 46 – THE SONGWRITERS 2

More songwriters for you to identify – who are credited with writing these songs:

1. *Bony Moronie*

2. *Great Balls Of Fire*

3. *At The Hop*

4. *Party Doll*

5. *Halfway To Paradise*

6. *Surfin' U.S.A*

7. *Jailhouse Rock*

8. *Save The Last Dance For Me*

9. *Only The Lonely*

10. *Rock Around The Clock*

QUIZ 47 – U.K. NUMBER ONES

Who had the first number one hits with the following songs in the U.K.?

1. *Dream Lover*

2. *Why Do Fools Fall In Love*

3. *Young Love*

4. *Yes Tonight Josephine*

5. *When*

6. *It's Only Make Believe*

7. *It's All In The Game*

8. *Only Sixteen*

9. *Blue Moon*

10. *Poetry In Motion*

QUIZ 48 - THE GROUPS

Ten questions on some of the pioneering rock 'n' roll groups:

1. Which band, formed from two members of The Robins, had a string of hits including *Young Blood*, *Poison Ivy* and *Along Came Jones*?

2. Which Canadian vocal group had hits with *Little Darlin'* and *The Stroll* and contrary to popular belief didn't have Tom Hanks' father as lead singer?

3. Which fabulous exponent of doo-wop had a 1959 hit with a cover version of *I Only Have Eyes For You*?

4. Which female group had a 1960 hit with *Will You Still Love Me Tomorrow*, a 1961 hit with *Baby It's You*, and a 1962 hit with *Soldier Boy*?

5. Which vocal group had a 1954 hit with *Sincerely*, their first record on the Chess Record label?

6. Which group had a number one hit with the Rodgers and Hart classic *Blue Moon* on both sides of the Atlantic?

7. What is the name of the highly successful vocal group that had a myriad of formations but was originally formed to back Clyde McPhatter?

8. With hits such as *Walk Like A Man*, *Rag Doll*, *Big Girls Don't Cry* and *Sherry* what is this enduring group?

9. What is the name of the group most closely associated with Dion DiMucci?

10. Which influential group had a 1959 hit with *Love Potion No. 9*?

QUIZ 49 – SAM PHILLIPS

One of the most influential men in the recording, production and early promotion of rock 'n' roll - try answering these questions on Sam Phillips:

1. In which southern state was Sam born in 1923?

2. What business did Sam open in Memphis on January 3 1950?

3. Although recorded by Sam, on which record label was *Rocket 88* released?

4. What was the record label that Sam started up in 1952?

5. Who was the local radio personality and assistant to Sam that first welcomed Elvis into the studio to supposedly record a record for his mother, and was so impressed that she insisted that Sam should call him back to the studio?

6. In 1955 Sam launched the WHER radio station, what was unusual about it?

7. Of whom did Sam supposedly say 'you play (the piano) with a white man's right hand and a black man's left, I'm gonna make you a star'?

8. Sam made stars of a host of rock 'n' roll performers including a session pianist who had a gold disc from a 1960 release *Lonely Weekends* - who was he?

9. To whom did Sam sell Sun Records in 1969?

10. Sam was an early investor in which Memphis hotel chain that would subsequently prove to have been a very shrewd gamble?

QUIZ 50 – GENERAL KNOWLEDGE 5

Another mix of questions to test your knowledge:

1. Which British rock 'n' roller is the only singer in the history of music to have a number 1 U.K. hit in the 1950s, 1960s, 1970s, 1980s and 1990s?

2. Where was Buddy Holly's last performance?

3. What was the sequel to the 1973 film *That'll Be The Day*?

4. Who played the iconic piano riff on Jackie Brenston and the Delta Cats' *Rocket 88*?

5. Whose autobiography was titled *Go, Cat, Go*?

6. Who had a number 3 hit in the U.K. in 1961 with *Take Good Care Of My Baby*?

7. Which legend did John Paramor play in the 1985 film *Shout! The Story of Johnny O'Keefe*?

8. Along with Elvis, who were the other two original Blue Moon Boys?

9. With which cover of a Pink song did Shakin' Stevens return to the U.K. charts in 2005?

10. George Harrison, Jeff Lynne, Bob Dylan, Tom Petty and which rock 'n' roll pioneer made up The Travelling Wilburys?

QUIZ 51 – ANAGRAMS 4

Some more rock 'n' roll performers to decipher:

1. Worth burn

2. Bide oddly

3. Jewellery Sire

4. Moo Cakes

5. Handball ark

6. Shoot Jinny

7. Silky Conner

8. Child rattlier

9. Cher Ruby KC

10. Braver ankle

QUIZ 52 – DEL SHANNON

Ten choice questions on Del Shannon:

1. What was Del Shannon's real name?

2. With which record label did Del sign in July 1960?

3. In Del's band was Max Crook - what instrument is Crook credited with inventing?

4. Del's first single release was a smash international hit - what was it?

5. Del's follow up single was a number 5 hit in the States and a number 6 in the U.K. - what was it?

6. Del's success continued, especially in the U.K. - his third single *So Long Baby* went to number 10 in the charts and his fourth single *Hey! Little Girl* went to number 2. On what album did the latter single appear?

7. On October 17 1962 Del had another number 2 hit in the U.K. with *Swiss Maid*, what song was on the B side?

8. Which self-penned song gave Del his final top ten hit in both the States and the U.K.?

9. Which 1968 album release of Del's took him away from rock 'n' roll to embrace psychedelia and with it brought him critical acclaim?

10. Del passed away on February 8 1990, what caused his death?

QUIZ 53 - INSTRUMENTALS

Who had hits with the following instrumentals:

1. *Walk Don't Run*

2. *Telstar*

3. *Sleep Walk*

4. *On The Rebound*

5. *Nutrocker*

6. *The Swag*

7. *Green Onions*

8. *Honky Tonk*

9. *Wipe Out*

10. *Tequila*

QUIZ 54 – ROCK 'N' ROLL CHRISTMAS

Christmas wouldn't be Christmas without rock 'n' roll:

1. What Christmas themed song did Elvis take to number 7 in the U.K. charts in November 1957?

2. Who wrote *Blue Christmas*?

3. It was Brenda Lee's biggest selling song but on which of her albums did *Rockin' Around The Christmas Tree* first appear?

4. Who wrote *Run Rudolph Run*?

5. This was the last U.K. number one for second generation British rock 'n' roller Shakin' Stevens, what is it?

6. On what 1963 album did The Ronettes sing *Frosty The Snowman* and *I Saw Mommy Kissing Santa Claus*?

7. Which artist first recorded and had a hit with *Jingle Bell Rock*?

8. Which vocal group released the single *Rudolph The Red-Nosed Reindeer* coupled with *Shock-A-Doo* in 1956?

9. Whose version of *White Christmas* is heard on the soundtrack to the films *Home Alone* and *The Santa Clause*?

10. What blues Christmas song was on Chuck Berry's flip side to his 1958 single *Run Rudolph Run*?

QUIZ 55 – PAT BOONE

Perhaps one of the unlikeliest and least rock 'n' roll of performers to embrace the genre - try these questions on Pat Boone:

1. With which record label did Pat release most of his records in the 1950s and 1960s?

2. Pat's fourth single release gave him a number 7 hit in the U.K. and a number 1 in the States what was it?

3. Pat's only number 1 hit in the U.K. was *I'll Be Home* but what was on the B side?

4. Pat continued his success in the charts on both sides of the Atlantic with his follow up release, what was it?

5. In the U.S. charts Pat had a number 7 hit with *At My Home Door (Crazy Little Mama)*, which doo-wop group originally had a hit with it?

6. In 1957 Pat starred in two popular films, *April Love* – with which he had a hit with the title track, and which other?

7. Pat married Shirley Lee Foley in 1953 when they were both 19, which country music legend was her father?

8. Pat had a number 1 hit in the U.S. and a number 2 in the U.K. with *Love Letters in the Sand*, which band recorded the song for their first album for Warner Bros. Records?

9. What was Pat's final top ten hit on both sides of the Atlantic?

10. In which 1959 science fiction film that was Oscar nominated did Pat star alongside James Mason?

QUIZ 56 – NAME THE YEAR

Identify the year from the following clues:

1. Roy Orbison's *A Black and White Night* is filmed, Aretha Franklin is the first woman inducted into the Rock and Roll Hall of Fame, Chuck Berry receives a star on the Hollywood Walk of Fame.

2. *Baby Face* is published, bass player Bill Black is born, there is a general strike in Great Britain.

3. Elvis is inducted into the army, Chuck Berry releases the album *One Dozen Berrys,* the United Kingdom opens its first motorway.

4. Ricky Nelson stars in *Rio Bravo* alongside Dean Martin and John Wayne, Jimi Hendrix buys his first electric guitar, Cliff Richard's album *Cliff Sings* is released.

5. Sam Phillips records Howlin' Wolf's *How Many More Years*, Alan Freed uses the term rock 'n' roll over the radiowaves, Phil Collins is born.

6. The Toronto Rock 'n' Roll Revival was staged, Elvis returns to the stage in Las Vegas, Neil Armstrong walks on the moon.

7. Showaddywaddy release *Under The Moon Of Love*, Bruce Springsteen jumps the wall of Graceland in an attempt to see Elvis, former road manager of the Beatles Mal Evans is shot dead by Los Angeles police.

8. *Blueberry Hill* is published, Cliff Richard is born, Disney's Pinocchio is released.

9. Sam Cooke is shot dead, the first edition of *Top of the Pops* is broadcast on BBC Television, the start of Beatlemania.

10. Jim Morrison is found dead, Jerry Lee Lewis releases the album *Touching Home,* Joe Frazier defeats Muhammad Ali in Madison Square Garden.

QUIZ 57 – WANDA JACKSON

The Queen of Rockabilly – see what you know about Wanda Jackson:

1. Wanda's first chart success came in 1956 for Capitol Records with a song bearing the same title, but of no other real similarity to a later hit for Elvis - what was it?

2. In the following year, which of her releases was a massive hit in Japan though had little effect in the U.S. or U.K.?

3. What was Wanda's first hit on the U.S. Billboard Hot 100 chart having been released on her first album in 1958 but not released as a single until 1960?

4. In 1961 Wanda released her second album, what was it called?

5. On that second album she covered songs by Elvis and Buddy Holly amongst others - what was the Paul Anka penned, Buddy Holly song she covered?

6. In October 1961 the album *Right or Wrong* was released, again with several cover versions, and another of Elvis' who she had briefly dated in the mid 1950s - what was the Elvis track?

7. For which album did Wanda receive her first Grammy nomination?

8. In 2011 she released a record breaking album entitled *The Party Ain't Over*, what is the name of the lead singer of the White Stripes that she worked with on the album?

9. Which of Wanda's songs was featured on the soundtrack to the Guy Ritchie movie *RocknRolla*?

10. Her thirty first and final studio album was released in 2012, what is it called?

QUIZ 58 – NAME THE ANIMAL

Name the animal from the following clues:

1. An easy one to start - a hit for Big Mama Mae Thornton and Elvis

2. 1958 hit for Bobby Day

3. Bill Haley's third and final million selling single

4. *Earth Angel* was a massive hit, but the only hit, for this Doo-Wop group

5. 1958 release for the Everly Brothers that topped the U.S. Billboard Country chart and went to number 2 on the Hot 100

6. A much recorded song, it was a number 1 smash for The Tokens in 1961

7. Johnny Preston hit written by J.P. Richardson

8. Chester Arthur Burnett

9. 1953 recording by Rufus Thomas that was written by Joe Hill Louis and Sam Phillips (under the pseudonym Burns)

10. The B side to Chuck Berry's *Brown Eyed Handsome Man*

QUIZ 59 – WHOSE LINE IS IT?

Identify the songs from which the following lines come:

1. Oh let the sun shine bright on my happy summer home

2. Why do birds sing so gay? And lovers await the break of day

3. I screamed and I hollered, I was so hard pressed. I called the woman that I loved the best

4. I light up when you call my name and you know I'm gonna treat you right

5. Now here's a dance (wack-a-doo, wack-a-doo), everyone can do (wack-a-doo, wack-a-doo)

6. Just promise me darling your love in return, may this fire in my soul dear, forever burn

7. I stepped out the tub, put my feet on the floor, I wrapped the towel around me and I opened the door

8. Let me be your little dog, 'til your big dog come. When the big dog gets here, show him what this little puppy done

9. Here come Tuesday, oh hard Tuesday, I'm so tired got no time to play

10. Ev'ry morning about this time, she get me out of my bed a-crying

QUIZ 60 – GENERAL KNOWLEDGE 6

More questions of a mixed nature to answer:

1. Who were the Million Dollar Quartet?

2. Who had a 1962 number 1 hit in the States with *Johnny Angel*?

3. Who was the influential vocal artist of the 1940s and 1950s who was the Epic Record label's most prolific artist?

4. Who was Frederick Albert Heath better known as?

5. What was Terry Dene's debut U.K. single that sold over 350,000 copies and went to number 18 in the U.K. charts?

6. What was the name of the 21 year old pilot who perished in the same crash as Buddy Holly?

7. For which 1985 film did Carl Perkins re-record *Blue Suede Shoes* along with Slim Jim Phantom and Lee Rocker?

8. Which 1980 musical comedy film starring Meatloaf gave Roy Orbison a cameo appearance?

9. In 1959 Tommy Steele had a number 5 U.K. hit with which very 'unrock 'n' roll' song?

10. Who wrote the humorous 'year in the life' style book *The Boys Of Summer – A Rock 'n' Roll Nightmare With Showaddywaddy*?

QUIZ 61 – NEIL SEDAKA

Ten questions on one of those pioneers of rock 'n' roll that is often overlooked:

1. From which country did both Neil's parents emigrate to the United States in 1910?

2. Neil was a founder member of which 50s group, but left before they were to have any success in the charts?

3. What was Neil's debut single release for R.C.A. that gave him a number 14 hit in the States?

4. Neil's second release for R.C.A. didn't have as much impact in the U.S. but gave him a number 9 hit in the U.K.. What was it?

5. As a 13 year old who was Neil introduced to with whom he would go on to write a string of hits?

6. Which song gave Neil his first top ten hit in the U.S.?

7. In 1961 Neil released *Calendar Girl* but what song was on the flip side?

8. On the 1964 album *3 Great Guys,* Neil shared the vinyl with which other two performers?

9. Neil also worked as a session musician - on which 1959 Bobby Darin hit is his piano playing heard?

10. For whom were Neil's co-penned songs *Another Sleepless Night, What Am I Gonna Do* and *All The Words In The World* hits?

QUIZ 62 – ALBUM TITLES 2

Some more studio albums for you to identify the artists:

1. *Encore* (1958)

2. *Ol' Blue Suede's Back* (1978)

3. *Right or Wrong* (1961)

4. *Mr 'Personality'* (1959)

5. *Crepes and Drapes* (1979)

6. *Promised Land* (1975)

7. *The Tra-La Days Are Over* (1973)

8. *I Remember Buddy Holly* (1963)

9. *Rockin' The Blues* (1958)

10. *Rock 'n' Roll Juvenile* (1979)

QUIZ 63 – BRITISH COVER VERSIONS

With the British rock 'n' roll revival of the 1970s, can you answer the following questions on the subsequent cover versions that received another breath of life:

1. What Ricky Nelson hit did Shakin' Stevens revive in 1983 resulting in a number 11 hit on the U.K. charts?

2. What Kalin Twins number 1 hit did Showaddywaddy record taking it to number 3 in the U.K. charts?

3. Which British band covered Gene Chandler's 1962 hit *Duke of Earl* taking it to number 6 in the U.K. charts in 1979?

4. The Jets got to number 25 in the U.K. charts in 1981 with *Yes, Tonight Josephine* but who had the original number 1 hit in 1957?

5. Which band had a 1980 number 4 hit in the U.K. with a cover of The Crickets' *When You Ask About Love*?

6. With what song, previously recorded by Carl Mann, Brenda Lee and Johnny Preston amongst others, did Alvin Stardust have a number 4 hit in the U.K.?

7. Which British rockers had a 1984 U.K. hit with the Dion hit *The Wanderer*?

8. Which Smiley Lewis song did Dave Edmunds have a 1970 smash number 1 hit with?

9. With what Crickets' song did Mud have a number 1 hit in the U.K. charts in 1975?

10. Who covered the Brenda Lee hit *Rockin' Around The Christmas Tree* in 1987 to raise funds for Comic Relief?

QUIZ 64 – WHO SAID THAT?

Ten great quotes - identify who said them or who they said them about:

1. Who famously called Chuck Berry 'The Shakespeare of rock 'n' roll'?

2. Who wrote: 'Buddy Holly and the Crickets were the template for all the rock band that followed'?

3. Who pointed to Fats Domino and said 'that's the real king of rock and roll'?

4. Who said 'if there were no Carl Perkins, there would be no Beatles'?

5. Who said 'rock 'n' roll has no beginning and no end for it is the very pulse of life itself'?

6. Who said 'I met Ray Charles at 14, and he was 16. But he was like a hundred years older than me'?

7. Which 80s pop star said 'Cliff Richard is, in my opinion, one of Britain's finest singers technically and emotionally. I've been a fan since Living Doll'?

8. Who said 'Elvis may be the King of Rock 'n' Roll, but I am the Queen'?

9. Who said 'Nothing affected me until I heard Elvis. Without Elvis, there would be no Beatles'?

10. Which lead singer of the band Ten Years After said 'My all-time favourite rock 'n' roll players were Scotty Moore, Chuck Berry and Franny Beecher'?

QUIZ 65 – IT'S A BOY THING!

Identify the boy's name from the following song clues:

1. Bobby Darin took this killer to the top of the charts both sides of the Atlantic in 1959.

2. LaVern Baker introduced the world to this hero in 1956.

3. Ray Charles said that he had to hit the road.

4. Lloyd Price told us that he shot Billy with a forty four.

5. Johnny Otis said that he could do the hand jive, even with his feet.

6. According to Pat Boone he was very nippy and had to get home quickly.

7. Del Shannon took his hat off to him because he broke his ex-girlfriend's heart.

8. Richard Berry penned song and release that gave the Kingsmen a huge 1963 hit.

9. Original title and song for *King Creole* that was cut but still recorded by Elvis.

10. He lived in Louisiana close to New Orleans.

QUIZ 66 – BRENDA LEE

Ten questions on the dynamic force that is Brenda Lee:

1. How old was Brenda when she recorded *Dynamite*?

2. That minor hit coupled with her diminutive stature gave her a lifelong nickname, what is it?

3. In October 1958 Brenda recorded a song that wouldn't be released until April of the following year, then wouldn't give her a hit until January 1961 when it got to 12 in the U.K. charts. What was the song?

4. What song written by Ronnie Self gave Brenda a number 4 hit both sides of the Atlantic in 1960?

5. In the 1960s she had more U.S. chart hits with 47 than any artist apart from Elvis, The Beatles and which other performer?

6. Which 1958 recording of Brenda's has sold over 25 million copies?

7. Which song, recorded by Brenda in 1960 was her first gold single, reached number 1 in the U.S. and number 12 in the U.K. and is regarded as her signature tune?

8. Which song was Brenda's top placed U.K. single in her career, getting to number 3, but was not released as a single in the States?

9. In 1962 Brenda toured West Germany and performed at the Star Club in Hamburg, which band opened for her?

10. In 1984 Brenda had a hit single in the U.S. with the Ray Charles classic *Halleluyah, I Love You So*, who did she duet with on the song?

QUIZ 67 – ANAGRAMS 5

Decipher these anagrams to find ten rock 'n' roll classic songs:

1. Hagen alert

2. Choosy Lad

3. Pigmy tuggers adoree

4. Islet slitter

5. Even the Aegean

6. Devon leggy limp

7. Aaren knows towelling

8. Gillette shoot Delmor

9. Tinkle awhile

10. Nursing dancer

QUIZ 68 – IT'S ALL ABOUT THE NOSTALGIA

Identify these nostalgic trips back to the golden age of rock 'n' roll:

1. A 1973 film directed by George Lucas and starring Harrison Ford, Richard Dreyfus and Ron Howard from which came a knockout soundtrack album.

2. Michael J Fox and Christopher Lloyd star in this 1985 masterpiece that sees the young Fox perform *Johnny B Goode* and a cameo from Huey Lewis.

3. Running from 1974 to 1984 this American sitcom was filled with classic tunes and introduced us to Henry Winkler's Fonz.

4. Starring Scott Bakula this was a television series that had an episode titled *Memphis Melody* in which the hero jumped back to July 3 1954 resulting in him impersonating Elvis.

5. A 1994 hit film starring Tom Hanks that followed his character's eventful life, with a soundtrack that sold over 12 million copies.

6. A 1987 classic movie starring Patrick Swayze and Jennifer Grey that had Bruce Channel, The Contours, The Ronettes and The Four Seasons all featuring on the soundtrack.

7. This 1990 Johnny Depp musical, romantic comedy set in the 1950s sees the cast perform classic numbers from the period such as *Sh-Boom, A Teenage Prayer, Gee* and *The Naughty Lady of Shady Lane*.

8. A British television light drama series based in Yorkshire and set in the early 1960s that drew heavily on rock 'n' roll and pop hits for its soundtrack, even utilising a Buddy Holly hit for its title.

9. A 1988 John Waters film starring Divine, Ricki Lake, Sonny Bono and Debbie Harry that took the viewer back to the sights and sounds of 1963.

10. Tobey Maguire and Reese Witherspoon star in this 1998 film with a soundtrack that includes *Be-Bop-A-Lula*, where two siblings are transported back to a 1950s television show.

QUIZ 69 – ONE HIT WONDERS

With which song did the following make their immortality then sink into obscurity, making them true 'One Hit Wonders':

1. Maurice Williams and the Zodiacs

2. Ernie K-Doe

3. The Teddy Bears

4. Bruce Channel

5. The Hollywood Argyles

6. Mark Dinning

7. The Silhouettes

8. Frankie Ford

9. Bobby Day

10. Ronald and Ruby

QUIZ 70 – GENERAL KNOWLEDGE 7

Ten more questions on a variety of rock 'n' roll subjects:

1. How did saxophone legend King Curtis die on August 13 1971?

2. Who was the longest serving member of The Drifters?

3. Which member of The Crickets released the single *Real Wild Child* under the pseudonym Ivan?

4. Apart from Buddy Holly, Big Bopper and Ritchie Valens, which other two music acts were advertised on the Winter Dance Party of 1959?

5. In which film did Elvis star with Nancy Sinatra?

6. A hugely influential figure to Fats Domino and Huey 'Piano' Smith, who was Henry Roeland 'Roy' Byrd better known as?

7. On September 14 1968 what tragedy befell Roy Orbison?

8. How was Lejzor Szmuel Czyz better known?

9. Born in Durham in the U.K. in 1937 what was the name of the eccentric piano player that played with Screaming Lord Sutch and the Savages and was known to sometimes destroy his piano with an axe as part of his performance?

10. Who had the original hit in 1957 of *Dedicated to the One I Love* that went to number 13 in the U.S. R&B charts?

QUIZ 71 – THE SONGWRITERS 3

Who is credited with penning the following songs:

1. *Sweet Nothin's*

2. *Reet Petite*

3. *It's Late*

4. *I Just Want To Make Love To You*

5. *Good Rockin' Tonight*

6. *Rock 'n' Roll Is Here To Stay*

7. *Charlie Brown*

8. *Too Much*

9. *See You Later, Alligator*

10. *Love Is Strange*

QUIZ 72 – THE DRIFTERS

A much changed line-up over the decades, but The Drifters remain one of the most successful vocal groups of all time, have a go at these questions on them:

1. The original Drifters were formed as a backing group for Clyde McPhatter who had formerly been singing with which vocal group?

2. As Clyde McPhatter and The Drifters what was the first single they released in 1953 which got to number 3 in the U.S. R&B charts?

3. A future hit for both Johnnie Ray (a number 1 in the U.K.) and Elvis, what song were The Drifters the first to record?

4. Their follow up release would give them a number 21 hit on the U.S. national charts, written by McPhatter and Jerry Wexler, what was it?

5. At the end of 1954 they released their version of a Bing Crosby classic which strongly influenced Elvis' 1957 version, what was the song?

6. Who was the manager of The Drifters that through the various changes of personnel held onto the name?

7. In 1958 the original Drifters were sacked and members of which group, which included Ben E King, were hired as replacements?

8. With Ben E King singing lead, the group had a U.S. national number 1 in 1959, what was the song?

9. The Drifters would have two number 2 hits in the U.K., the first was *Save The Last Dance For Me* in 1960, what was the second and in what year?

10. When Ben E King left the band, who joined and sang lead on such hits as *Some Kind Of Wonderful*, *On Broadway* and *Up On The Roof*?

QUIZ 73 – ROCK 'N' ROLL MUSICALS

How well do you know the stage shows built around rock 'n' roll?

1. During its original run on Broadway what rock 'n' roll show included in its cast, at one time or another, Richard Gere, Jeff Conaway, Patrick Swayze and John Travolta?

2. Who wrote and starred in the homage to 1950s culture *The Rocky Horror Show*?

3. Premiering at the Edinburgh International Festival in 1971 which early Tim Rice and Andrew Lloyd Webber musical includes an Elvis-like Pharoah?

4. Which highly fictionalized account of a 1956 impromptu recording session opened on Broadway in 2010 and on London's West End in 2011?

5. What rock 'n' roll musical opened at London's Victoria Palace Theatre on October 12 1989 and gave 5140 performances in the West End?

6. On which Shakespeare play did Bob Carlton loosely base his rock 'n' roll jukebox musical *Return to the Forbidden Planet*?

7. What was the name of the musical revue that opened on Broadway in 1995 that showcased 39 songs written by Jerry Leiber and Mike Stoller?

8. What title did Alan Bleasdale choose for his 1985 play with music that starred Martin Shaw as Elvis at The Phoenix Theatre in London's West End?

9. What was the name of the American musical that opened on Broadway in 2011 that tells the story of Scepter Records and features a host of Shirelles hits?

10. Which popular jukebox musical set between 1957 and 1963 opened at London's Savoy Theatre in July 2009 moved to The Playhouse Theatre in January 2010 and then between October 2012 and January 2013 was at the Wyndham's Theatre?

QUIZ 74 – JOHNNY CASH

He was the man in black and one of the most influential artists of the twentieth century in rock 'n' roll, country and blues - try these questions on him:

1. What name was Johnny Cash given on his birth?

2. He began to use the name Johnny when signing for Sun Records, but when did he first have to adopt a first name of John?

3. What was the first single that Johnny released on the Sun Record label?

4. Johnny's first U.S. national charting single was *I Walk The Line* but what song was on the flip side?

5. What was the title given to Johnny's debut album release?

6. What was Johnny's original backing band at Sun named?

7. Which song, written by Jack Clement, gave Johnny his third number 1 hit on the U.S. Country charts in 1958?

8. By and large how did Johnny introduce himself on stage?

9. The co-writer of *Ring Of Fire*, who did Johnny marry on March 1 1968?

10. Johnny would have two U.K. top ten hits - *A Thing Called Love* was one, what was the other?

QUIZ 75 – IN THE MOVIES 2

Another selection of questions on rock 'n' roll stars on the big screen:

1. In which 1962 film starring Helen Shapiro and Craig Douglas did Del Shannon have a cameo along with Chubby Checker and Gene Vincent among others?

2. Which 1973 British film was Cliff Richard's last starring role?

3. In which Elvis film did Mary Tyler-Moore co-star?

4. Which teen rocker starred in and had a hit with the title song of 1959's *Hound-Dog Man*?

5. In which 1962 Don Siegel directed film did Bobby Darin share the screen with Steve McQueen and James Coburn?

6. Which female number 1 hitmaker in the United States starred with Peter Noone in the 1966 film *Hold On!*

7. In which 1965 British film starring David Hemmings and Steve Marriott did Jerry Lee Lewis make an appearance with The Nashville Teens?

8. What was the title of the 1967 film which gave Roy Orbison his only starring role as an actor?

9. Which Sun recording star starred in the 1961 film *Five Minutes To Live*?

10. In which 1967 horror film did Neil Sedaka make a cameo appearance?

QUIZ 76 – WHAT'S THE NUMBER?

All the answers are numbers ….. :

1. The number of flights of stairs that Eddie Cochran had to ascend

2. Sam Cooke sang about being only this age

3. Elvis' A side to *I Got Stung* that implied how many nights of sin he wanted

4. The cell block number that the Robins sang about in the Leiber and Stoller composition

5. The number of minutes that Jerry Lee Lewis and The Dominoes both claimed they could make love for in song

6. The number of hours past midnight that Johnny 'Guitar' Watson was

7. How long Chuck Berry was giving his girlfriend to return home in his follow up single to *Maybellene*

8. The number of tons that Tennessee Ernie Ford, The Coasters and even Elvis sang about

9. The number of Jackie Brenston's car

10. After a nuclear catastrophe the number of women that remained according to the Bill Haley song

QUIZ 77 – TOMMY STEELE

He was one of the U.K.'s first rock 'n' rollers, what do you know about him?

1. A week after Guy Mitchell was at number 1 in the U.K. charts, Tommy Steele would be at number 1 with the same song in 1957, what was it?

2. What was the name of Tommy's group that are credited on his early releases?

3. Who came up with Tommy's surname?

4. On which early album of Tommy's did he include the songs *Elevator Rock*, *A Handful Of Songs*, *Cannibal Post* and *Butterfingers*?

5. What was Tommy's follow-up top twenty hit to his number 1 in 1957?

6. Released in 1957 what was the first film that Tommy appeared in when he gives a cameo?

7. With which record label did Tommy release all of his U.K. top forty hit singles?

8. With what song would Tommy spend eleven weeks in the U.K. charts in 1958 with a top position of number 3?

9. Tommy is a respected painter and sculptor, which of his works can be found in Stanley Street in Liverpool?

10. In 2008 who did Tommy say he secretly gave a tour of London to back in 1958 or 1959?

QUIZ 78 – ON THIS DAY 2

In rock 'n' roll music history, identify the importance of these dates:

1. March 9 1974 – which British rocker was at number 1 in the U.K. charts with *Jealous Mind*?

2. December 20 1973 – which singer, who had a 1959 number 1, died on this date at the age of just 37?

3. May 10 1935 – which rock 'n' roll singer and songwriter who had hits with *Short Fat Fannie* and *Dizzy Miss Lizzy* was born?

4. November 17 1962 – The Four Seasons started a five week run at number 1 on the U.S. charts with what song?

5. November 9 1955 – which related duo made their first studio recordings at the Old Tulane Hotel studios in Nashville?

6. July 19 1954 – who signed with Sun Records and gave his notice at his day job at The Crown Electric Company?

7. May 22 1958 – who flew in to Heathrow Airport from the United States with his teenage bride?

8. June 4 1942 – which record label was launched in the United States by Glenn Wallichs which would release records by Gene Vincent, Eddie Cochran, Bobby Darin and Tina Turner amongst many others?

9. July 6 1957 – which hugely important meeting took place between two young rockers at the Woolton Church Parish Fete in Liverpool?

10. October 9 1988 – which influential guitarist on such hits as *Be-Bop-A-Lula* died of a heart attack?

QUIZ 79 – SAM COOKE

He had the most perfect voice in soul, but was also a pioneer of rock 'n' roll, here are ten questions on the phenomenal Sam Cooke:

1. Sam's first hit was written by him and released on the Keen record label, what was it?

2. The next song that would give him a hit in the U.K. was *Only Sixteen* which went to number 23 in 1959, but who would have a number 1 hit in the U.K. with the song?

3. Sam's *Wonderful World* gave him a number 27 hit in the U.K. in 1960, but in what year was it rereleased and went to number 2?

4. What was Sam's second top ten hit in the U.S. Hot 100 and first top ten hit in the U.K. charts?

5. To which record label did Sam sign in January 1960?

6. The following year Sam started his own record label, what was it called?

7. Released in April 1962 what was the name of the album that went to 74 in the U.S. album charts and gave him a top ten single of the same name both sides of the Atlantic?

8. Recorded in 1963 but not released until 1985, where was Sam's live album recorded which is now regarded as one of the best of its kind?

9. Getting to number 30 on the U.K. charts, what was Sam's last hit in the 1960s in the U.K.?

10. Sam was shot and killed at the Hacienda Motel in Los Angeles on December 11 1964, how old was he?

QUIZ 80 – GENERAL KNOWLEDGE 8

More questions on a range of topics

1. Perhaps the first band to record a rock 'n' roll record but what band was Jackie Brenston and the Delta Cats in actual fact?

2. What was the name of the 1973 documentary/concert film that featured performances from Chuck Berry, Fats Domino, Bo Diddley, Bill Haley, The Five Satins and Little Richard amongst others?

3. Who had a 1955 number 16 hit in the U.S. charts with the Otis Williams and the Charms' song *Two Hearts, Two Kisses (Make One Love)*?

4. What was the name of the band that Huey 'Piano' Smith formed in 1957 with whom he would have a minor hit with *Rockin' Pneumonia and the Boogie Woogie Flu*?

5. What's the title of the 1996 Tom Hanks directed film that told the fictional story of a 1960s rock 'n' roll band called The Oneders who become one hit wonders?

6. With what song did Eddie Cochran have a number 15 hit on the U.K. charts in 1961?

7. On which American television show did Elvis Presley have to sing to a basset hound wearing a top hat in 1956?

8. Violating what Act caused Chuck Berry to serve twenty months in prison at the beginning of the 1960s?

9. A hit for Lulu in 1964 who wrote and originally recorded *Shout* in 1959?

10. Which British guitarist counts amongst his many achievements recording with The Crickets on three albums and acting as the musical director for the Everly Brothers' 1983 reunion concert?

QUIZ 81 – U.S. NUMBER ONES

What were the first number one hits on the Billboard chart for the following artists:

1. The Platters

2. Elvis Presley

3. The Everly Brothers

4. Sam Cooke

5. Danny and the Juniors

6. The Champs

7. The Coasters

8. Lloyd Price

9. Frankie Avalon

10. Chubby Checker

QUIZ 82 – BOBBY VEE

Ten questions on one of the most popular young artists of the early 1960s:

1. What was Bobby's real name?

2. Bobby's career was effectively launched at the Moorhead Armory, Minnesota when he performed there on February 3 1959 as a fifteen year old, why was he suddenly thrust into the spotlight?

3. His first single was soon rushed out on the Soma record label, written by himself, what was it?

4. Which record label subsequently gave him a recording contract after the local success of his first single?

5. Bobby's first single recorded for the new label was actually a cover version of *What Do You Want?* a number 1 in the U.K. for which British performer?

6. Which Clovers' hit did Bobby subsequently cover to give himself a top ten hit in the U.S.?

7. What song, which went to number 4, was Bobby's first showing on the U.K. charts?

8. According to Bobby's 1962 album which went to number 2 in the U.K. charts, who did he meet?

9. Bobby featured in the 1961 film *Swingin' Along* performing his hit *More Than I Can Say*, what song was Ray Charles seen performing in the film?

10. Which song by Carole King and Gerry Goffin did Bobby take to the top of the U.S. charts in 1961 and to number 3 in the U.K.?

QUIZ 83 – ALBUM FILLERS

On which album would you find the following songs:

1. A 1957 release that included *Drown In My Own Tears, Mess Around, I Got A Woman* and *Hallelujah I Love Her So*

2. An album from 1956 with the tracks *Poor Me, Ain't It A Shame, Bo Weevil* and *The Fat Man*

3. Another album from 1956, this one had *Rockin' Thru The Rye, Choo Choo Ch'Boogie, Rudy's Rock* and *A Rockin' Little Tune*

4. A 1963 soundtrack album that included *Foot Tapper, Dancing Shoes, The Next Time* and *Bachelor Boy*

5. A live album from 1963 included *La Bamba, What I'd Say, Unchain My Heart* and *If I Had A Hammer*

6. Released in August 1956 this included *Jezebel, Ain't She Sweet, Up A Lazy River* and *Wedding Bells (Are Breaking Up That Old Gang Of Mine)*

7. A classic album from 1960 that had *That's Love, Don't Leave Me This Way, Don't Say it's Over* and *My Advice?*

8. A 1957 album crammed with quality songs like *Blueberry Hill, True Love, Mean Woman Blues* and *Got A Lot O' Livin' To Do*

9. A 1963 album that included *Heartbreak Hotel, Blue Suede Shoes, Don't Be Cruel* and *Love Me Tender*

10. Originally released in 1959 on Lion Records, this had *Elmer The Elephant, Harold The Hippo, Pinky The Penguin* and *Oscar The Octopus*

QUIZ 84 – NAME THE INSTRUMENT 2

With which instrument would you identify the following maestros :

1. Hal Blaine

2. Ray Pohlman

3. Hank Marvin

4. Glen Hardin

5. Danny Flores

6. James Fuller

7. Jackie Brenston

8. Bob Bogle

9. Carol Kaye

10. Jimmy Van Eaton

QUIZ 85 – THE CRICKETS

It wasn't just about Buddy Holly, here are some questions on the band that kept the music alive:

1. Who were the original members of The Crickets?

2. What was the name of the band's debut album?

3. A number 10 hit in the U.S. and a number 3 in the U.K., what was The Crickets' second single release?

4. What was the final single release by The Crickets when Buddy Holly was a member of the band?

5. On the band's 1959 single *Love's Made A Fool Of You* – a U.K. number 26 hit, who took the lead vocals?

6. The band returned to the U.K. charts in 1960 with *More Than I Can Say* a song written by Sonny Curtis and Jerry Allison. A year later Bobby Vee would have a bigger hit with it taking it to number 4, but who, in 1980 would take it to number 2?

7. Which other former lead singer of The Crickets (albeit for a short time) was also killed in a plane crash?

8. Which superb album did the band release on December 4 1960 which included the first recording of Sonny Curtis' *I Fought The Law*?

9. Reaching number 21 in the U.K. charts in 1964 what was their last charting hit in the U.K. or the States?

10. Who, as of Christmas 2020 is the sole surviving member of the original Crickets?

QUIZ 86 - THE LIVE ALBUMS

Whose performances were released on the following fantastic live albums:

1. *Twistin' Knights at the Roundtable* (1962)

2. *In Concert at Pacoima Jr. High* (1960)

3. *At San Quentin* (1969)

4. *Aloha from Hawaii via Satellite* (1973)

5. *At The Copa* (1964)

6. *Live at The International, Las Vegas* (1970)

7. *In Person, Recorded Live at Mr. Lucky's* (1969)

8. *Live at Fillmore Auditorium* (1967)

9. *Live at The Olympia* (2014)

10. *In Concert at the Troubadour, 1969* (1969)

QUIZ 87 – SONGS THAT INSPIRED THE FILM TITLE

Name these films that all got their title from a rock 'n' roll classic:

1. A 1986 film starring Kathleen Turner who is transported back to her high school year of 1960

2. Based on a Stephen King novella entitled *The Body*, this is a coming of age film that stars Kiefer Sutherland, River Phoenix and Corey Feldman

3. A 1988 film starring Tuesday Weld and David Keith about a fictional kidnapping of Elvis

4. A John Hughes written romcom from 1987 that starred Mary Stuart Masterson, Eric Stoltz and Lea Thompson

5. Actually a remake of a 1960 French classic which had nothing to do with the Jerry Lee Lewis recording of the same name, this 1983 Richard Gere film made full use of the song in its soundtrack

6. A 1995 romcom starring Matthew Modine, Randy Quaid and Paul Reiser as three divorced men trying to deal with the complications of relationships

7. A forgettable Sandra Bullock film from 1992 that uses a Coasters hit both as its title and approximate plot

8. A 1989 thriller starring Al Pacino, Ellen Barkin and John Goodman that utilises a 1959 song by Phil Philips as its title

9. A 1973 film starring David Essex and also featuring Ringo Starr, Billy Fury and Keith Moon

10. Starring Richard Gere and Julia Roberts …….

QUIZ 88 – THE WRITERS

Who wrote the following exceptional histories on rock 'n' roll and its biggest names:

1. *Last Train To Memphis* (1994)

2. *Be My Baby: How I Survived Mascara, Miniskirts and Madness* (1990)

3. *Blues All Around Me* (1996)

4. *Great Balls Of Fire* (1982)

5. *Awopbopaloobop Alopbamboom: The Golden Age Of Rock* (1969)

6. *Rave On: The Biography of Buddy Holly* (1996)

7. *The History of Rock & Roll – Volume One 1920–1963* (2016)

8. *Takin' Back My Name* (1999)

9. *Crazy Man, Crazy* (2019)

10. *Making Your Memories with Rock & Roll and Doo-Wop – The Music and Artists of the 1950s and Early 1960s* (2016)

QUIZ 89 – SHAKIN' STEVENS

The U.K.'s top selling singles artist of the 1980s, Shakin' Stevens did much to energise and maintain interest in rock 'n' roll, here are 10 questions on the artist.

1. What is Shakin' Stevens real name?

2. With which group did Shakin' Stevens first perform and release both singles and albums?

3. What was the Dave Edmunds produced album, their first, that they released in October 1970?

4. With which 60s recording artist did he share the Astoria Theatre stage in London's West End in the musical *Elvis*?

5. Which single release eventually gave Shakin' Stevens a hit record when it went to number 24 on the U.K. charts in 1980?

6. His first number 1 hit was *This Ole House*, but who had the number 1 hit on both sides of the Atlantic with the song in 1954?

7. What was the title of the album that he released in 1981 that went to the top of the U.K. album charts?

8. In 1982 he would have his third number 1 hit in the U.K., what was it?

9. In which 2005 ITV programme did Shakin' Stevens beat other contestants such as Chesney Hawkes and Carol Decker resulting in a rerelease of *This Ole House* and a number 20 hit in the U.K.?

10. What was the name of the well-received album that he released in 2016?

QUIZ 90 – GENERAL KNOWLEDGE 9

A final selection of general rock 'n' roll knowledge questions:

1. Which song, covered by Buddy Holly but originally from Elvis' *Jailhouse Rock* are the first lines: *You don't like crazy music, you don't like rockin' bands, you just wanna go to a movie show and sit there holdin' hands*

2. Which British band acted as Jerry Lee Lewis' group for several of his tours and performed with him at his famous 1964 Star Club engagements?

3. Collectively, as what were Gordon Stoker, Neal Matthews, Hoyt Hawkins and Ray Walker known?

4. Under what pseudonym did Jerry Lee Lewis record and release an instrumental version of *In The Mood* in 1960 on the Phillips International record label?

5. What was the 1987 documentary *Hail! Hail! Rock 'n' Roll* ostensibly celebrating?

6. What Lieber and Stoller song did Trini Lopez take to number 23 in the U.S. and number 35 in the U.K. charts in 1963?

7. Which female vocal group took the Beverly Ross and Julius Dixson song *Lollipop* to number 2 in the U.S. and number 6 in the U.K. charts?

8. Which country music legendary guitarist and vocalist was once a member of The Champs and The Beach Boys and played on recordings by The Everly Brothers, Bobby Vee, Ricky Nelson, Bobby Darin and Elvis?

9. Written by Ike Turner and released on the Tune Town record label in August 1958, which is the first appearance of Tina Turner on a record (under the name 'Little Ann')?

10. In topping the U.K. charts on November 25 1955 with *Rock Around The Clock* what single did Bill Haley and his Comets knock off the top spot?

QUIZ 91 – FIRST LINES 2

What songs are these the first lines of:

1. I was slippin' and slidin' with a long tall Sally, peekin' and a hidin', duck back in the alley

2. They asked me how I knew my true love was true

3. Arrested on charges of unemployment he was sitting in the witness stand

4. I'm gonna tell you how it's gonna be, you're gonna give your love to me

5. People see us everywhere they think you really care

6. The night was clear and the moon was yellow and the leaves came tumbling down

7. If you love me please don't tease if I can hold then let me squeeze

8. Old man rhythm is in my shoes it's no use to sittin' and a-singin' the blues

9. The best things in life are free but you can give them to the birds and bees

10. Let me tell you 'bout a girl I know, she's my baby and she lives next door

QUIZ 92 – STARS IN THEIR EYES

A selection of questions on film portrayals of rock 'n' roll's heroes:

1. Although factually weak, who gave an excellent performance as Buddy in the 1978 film *The Buddy Holly Story*?

2. A country star who lived the rock 'n' roll lifestyle and influenced so many rock 'n' rollers, who played Hank Williams in the 2015 biopic *I Saw The Light*?

3. A much maligned film, especially by its subject, who took the part of Jerry Lee Lewis in 1989's *Great Balls Of Fire*?

4. In which 1987 film did Brian Setzer get to portray his idol Eddie Cochran?

5. In 1979 Kurt Russell portrayed Elvis in the made for television film directed by John Carpenter simply titled *Elvis*, but in which film did Kurt Russell actually share screen time with Presley?

6. In which 1998 film that had a cameo by Little Richard, did Larenz Tate star as Frankie Lymon?

7. In the 2008 film *Cadillac Records* who played the role of Chuck Berry?

8. Which icon did Leon Preston Robinson portray on screen in a 2000 biopic?

9. Who took the lead role in the 2004 biopic of Ray Charles, *Ray*?

10. Who took the role of Ike Turner in the 1993 film *What's Love Got To Do With It*?

QUIZ 93 – THE STRAY CATS

The fabulous American rockabilly band that utilised the rock 'n' roll revival in the U.K. to gain their popularity and success. Ten quick questions on the boys:

1. Who comprise the Stray Cats?

2. On which rock 'n' roll film soundtracks from 1973 and 1974 are The Stray Cats featured, but are actually an unrelated band?

3. Which Welsh rocker produced their first studio album that was simply entitled *Stray Cats*?

4. It failed to chart in the U.S. but their first single was a number 9 hit in the U.K., what was it?

5. Their next two releases, like their first, both taken from their debut album, had success both sides of the Atlantic. *Rock This Town* was one, what was the other?

6. Their debut album in the U.S. went to number 2 in the album charts in 1982, what was it called?

7. Reaching number 5 on the Billboard Hot 100 and number 29 in the U.K. in 1983, what was the band's last meaningful hit?

8. Which former Bond girl and ex-wife of Peter Sellers did Slim Jim Phantom marry in 1984?

9. Formed in 1990 what is the full title of the BSO?

10. In 2019 the band released their first studio album for fifteen years, what is it called?

QUIZ 94 – WHOSE LINE IS IT? 2

More songs to identify from which the following lines come:

1. That long black train carry my baby and gone

2. Until one night she caught me right and now I'm on the run

3. I should have known it from the very start, this girl will leave me with a broken heart

4. Everybody was juiced, you can bet your soul, they did the boogie woogie with a steady roll

5. Knocked once, tried to tell them I'd been there, door slammed, hospitality's thin there

6. I want to go all the time, you'll be my love tonight, little darling let's walk, let's talk

7. She worries me so, if she'd leave us alone, we would have a happy home, sent from down below

8. The warden said 'come out with your hands in the air, if you don't stop this riot, you're all gonna get the chair'

9. Words are like rainbows, bright as the stars, they're always with you, wherever you are

10. And a city boy named Dan, had to prove who could run the fastest, to win Miss Lucy's hand

QUIZ 95 – 'COVERS' ALBUMS

Well after the first flush of rock 'n' roll, who released these (mostly) fabulous albums of rock 'n' roll covers:

1. Released in 1975 on the Apple label this was simply entitled *Rock 'n' Roll* and included such songs as *Stand By Me*, *Be-Bop-A-Lula*, *Peggy Sue* and *Bony Moronie*

2. Fantastic 1994 album entitled *Four Chords and Several Years Ago* which included *Mother-in-Law*, *Little Bitty Pretty One*, *Blue Monday* and *Good Morning Little School Girl*

3. Titled *Famous in the Last Century* and released in 2000 it included the songs *Roll Over Beethoven*, *Memphis Tennessee*, *Rave On!* and *Runaround Sue*

4. Released in 1973 this classic album is titled *Moondog Matinee* and includes *Ain't Got No Home*, *Mystery Train*, *The Great Pretender* and *Promised Land*

5. A 2016 album titled *Just …Fabulous Rock 'n' Roll* which included *Multiplication*, *Blue Suede Shoes*, *Cathy's Clown* and *Keep A-Knockin*

6. In 1976 this band released their 20th studio album titled *15 Big Ones* which included *Blueberry Hill*, *Chapel Of Love*, *Rock 'n' Roll Music* and *In The Still of the Night*?

7. A well-loved duo that released the 1995 album *Rock 'n' Roll Party* and the 2002 album *Rock 'n' Roll Knees Up*

8. This eponymous album of 1985 by Willie and The Poor Boys included *You Never Can Tell*, *Slippin' and Slidin'*, *Revenue Man* and *These Arms of Mine*, but who put this special band together of iconic musicians?

9. Released as *The Jukebox Years* in 2004 this is best ignored, it includes *Hello Mary Lou*, *All Shook Up*, *When* and *Three Steps To Heaven*

10. Released in the Soviet Union in 1988 but not until 1991 for the rest of the world, *Choba B CCCP* includes *Lucille*, *Twenty Flight Rock*, *Kansas City* and *That's All Right Mama*

QUIZ 96 – THE SONGWRITERS 4

Who is credited with penning the following songs:

1. *Hello Mary Lou*

2. *Heartbreak Hotel*

3. *Ooby Dooby*

4. *Be-Bop Baby*

5. *Peter Gunn*

6. *It's Only Make Believe*

7. *Raining In My Heart*

8. *Ubangi Stomp*

9. *Rip It Up*

10. *Rocket 88*

QUIZ 97 - SHOWADDYWADDY

One of the U.K.'s most successful rock 'n' roll revival groups, what do you know about them?

1. From which Midlands city did Showaddywaddy originate?

2. Showaddywaddy were originally formed by amalgamating two groups, what were the two groups?

3. On which ATV television show did the band appear in 1973 that effectively launched their career?

4. In the original band, because of the amalgamation of two bands, there were two drummers, who were they?

5. Who was the band's frontman and lead singer for almost 38 years until his retirement in 2011?

6. Their first single release after their success on ATV television went to number 2 in the U.K. charts in 1974, what was it?

7. The band would have a number 1 hit in 1976 with a Curtis Lee song, what was it?

8. The band's debut album was eponymous, what was their second album titled?

9. Reaching 37 in the U.K. charts in 1982 what was the band's last top 40 hit?

10. As of Christmas 2020 who is the current lead singer of Showaddywaddy?

QUIZ 98 - ELVIS

Questions on the man many call the King:

1. What was the first single that Elvis released on the Sun label?

2. How much did Sam Phillips receive from R.C.A. for Elvis' recording contract?

3. What was the follow up hit for Elvis after his number one in the States with *Heartbreak Hotel*?

4. What was Elvis' first number one in the U.K.?

5. Featuring the songs *(Let Me Be Your) Teddy Bear, Party* and *Got A Lot Of Livin' To Do*, what was the title of Elvis' second feature film?

6. What was the name of Elvis' longtime (in)famous manager?

7. What was the first film that Elvis made after being released by the army?

8. After *Good Luck Charm* in 1962, Elvis didn't have another number one in the States until 1969, what was that song that also gave him a number 2 hit in the U.K.?

9. As of Christmas 2020 how many number 1 hits has Elvis had in the U.K.?

10. What is Elvis' bestselling song in the U.K. with over 1.3 million sales and twice topping the U.K. charts – in 1960 and 2005?

QUIZ 99 – THREE STEPS TO HEAVEN

Which rock 'n' roll legends took their final bow on the following dates:

1. December 31 1985

2. February 9 1981

3. October 12 1971

4. December 11 1964

5. March 18 2017

6. August 24 2017

7. September 12 2003

8. June 10 2004

9. December 12 2007

10. August 16 1977

QUIZ 100 – IT'S STILL ROCK 'N' ROLL TO ME

Answer the following questions on the songs that prove that rock 'n' roll will never die!

1. Which Billy Joel song, written in the doo-wop style, gave him a number 14 hit in the U.S. and number 25 in the U.K. in 1984?

2. In 1979 Queen had a number 2 hit with a song that Freddie Mercury wrote as a tribute to the music of Elvis - what was it?

3. What Elton John song, an homage to the music he grew up listening to, gave him his first number 1 in the U.S.?

4. What song was recorded by Bob Seger and immortalised in the Tom Cruise film *Risky Business*?

5. Which British rock band had a 1983 hit with their original song *Twisting by the Pool*?

6. With which very rock 'n' roll song did George Michael have a massive international hit in 1987?

7. In 2006 Amy Winehouse released a whole album of songs that seemed to be an homage to the early rock 'n' roll girls groups of the 50s and 60s. What was the album called?

8. What was the name of the song and the album from which it came that was released by The Rolling Stones in 1974 giving them a number 10 hit?

9. Which 1982 cover of an Arrows song, by Joan Jett and the Blackhearts gave her a number 1 hit in the States and was later covered less successfully by Britney Spears?

10. What 2008 single, highly influenced by early 60s rock 'n' roll and soul, gave Duffy a number 1 hit on the U.K. charts?

THE ANSWERS

QUIZ 1 - NICE AND EASY DOES IT
1. Elvis Presley
2. Piano
3. Chuck Berry
4. The Crickets
5. The Big Bopper
6. Memphis, Tennessee
7. *The Blackboard Jungle*
8. Gene Vincent
9. Fats Domino
10. Little Richard

QUIZ 2 – THE BIRTH OF ROCK 'N' ROLL
1. Alan Freed in 1951
2. Louis Jordan
3. *Roll 'Em Pete*
4. Sister Rosetta Tharpe
5. *Good Rockin' Tonight*
6. Wynonie Harris
7. April 1949
8. *The Fat Man*
9. *That's All Right Mama*
10. *Rocket 88*

QUIZ 3 – ALAN FREED
1. The Moondog House
2. The Moondog Coronation Ball at the Cleveland Arena
3. *Rock, Rock, Rock!*
4. Alan Freed's Rock 'n' Roll Dance Party
5. *Mister Rock and Roll*
6. Because on the second episode black singer Frankie Lymon was seen dancing with a white girl.
7. Fuqua insisted that Freed was a co-writer, unlike Berry's insistence that he wasn't on *Maybellene*
8. Inciting to riot
9. Payola – the practice of taking payments (bribes) from record companies to play their records, for which it was proven he had done.
10. 43

QUIZ 4 – BORN TO ROCK 'N' ROLL
1. Jerry Lee Lewis
2. Duane Eddy
3. Eddie Cochran
4. Wee Willie Harris
5. Carl Perkins
6. Wanda Jackson
7. Marty Wilde

8. Brenda Lee
9. Johnny Burnette
10. Roy Orbison

QUIZ 5 – CHUCK BERRY
1. Charles Edward Anderson Berry
2. He was convicted of robbing three shops and stealing a car at gunpoint
3. Pianist Johnnie Johnson's (Johnnie would become Chuck's piano player in due course)
4. Muddy Waters
5. *Maybellene*
6. *Drifting Heart*
7. *After School Session*
8. *School Day (Ring! Ring! Goes The Bell)* peaked at 24 on June 27 1957
9. *You Never Can Tell*
10. *My Ding-a-ling*

QUIZ 6 – REAL NAMES
1. Little Richard
2. Billy Fury
3. Gene Vincent
4. Cliff Richard
5. Marty Wilde
6. Tommy Steele
7. Buddy Holly
8. Chubby Checker
9. Connie Francis
10. Ricky Valance

QUIZ 7 - ANAGRAMS
1. Frankie Lymon
2. Elvis Presley
3. Johnny Kidd
4. Fats Domino
5. Tommy Steele
6. Eddie Cochran
7. Screaming Lord Sutch
8. Wanda Jackson
9. Big Joe Turner
10. Vince Eager

QUIZ 8 – BILL HALEY
1. Highland Park, Michigan on July 6 1925
2. He was blind in the left eye, the optic nerve had been accidentally severed during an operation
3. Yodeling, he was dubbed Silver Yodeling Bill Haley
4. *Crazy Man, Crazy*

5. Bill Haley & His Comets
6. *Shake, Rattle and Roll*
7. *Rockin' Around The World*
8. *The Saints Rock 'n' Roll*
9. Rudy Pompilli the Comets' saxophonist
10. A heart attack

QUIZ 9 – FIRST LINES
1. *Don't Be Cruel* – Elvis Presley
2. *The Wanderer* – Dion and the Belmonts
3. *Blue Bayou* – Roy Orbison
4. *Johnny B Goode* – Chuck Berry
5. *Come A Little Bit Closer* – Jay and the Americans
6. *Speedy Gonzales* – Pat Boone
7. *Long Tall Sally* – Little Richard
8. *It'll Be Me* – Jerry Lee Lewis
9. *Shake, Rattle and Roll* – Big Joe Turner
10. *Teenager In Love* – Marty Wilde

QUIZ 10 – GENERAL KNOWLEDGE
1. Moondog or King of the Moondoggers (one he self-adopted for his radio broadcasts)
2. Sun Studios
3. *Western Movies*
4. Tommy Edwards
5. Conway Twitty
6. Four (*Whole Lotta Shakin'*, *Great Balls Of Fire*, *Breathless* and *What'd I Say*)
7. He drowned when his fishing boat was hit by a cabin cruiser and he was thrown into the water.
8. *Young Love*
9. Georgie Fame
10. Frankie Avalon

QUIZ 11 – EDDIE COCHRAN
1. None
2. Crest Records
3. *Skinny Jim*
4. *Untamed Youth*
5. Liberty Records
6. Jerry Capehart (who also managed Eddie)
7. *C'mon Everybody*/*Don't Ever Let Me Go*
8. *Three Stars*
9. *Poor Little Fool*
10. Jerry Allison and Sonny Curtis of The Crickets

QUIZ 12 - SKIFFLE
1. Lonnie Donegan
2. *Rock Island Line*
3. *Freight Train*
4. The Beatles
5. The Vipers
6. *Last Train To San Fernando*
7. *Six-Five Special*
8. The Bob Cort Skiffle Group
9. The 2i's Coffee Bar
10. The Rattlesnakes

QUIZ 13 - BIOPICS
1. Johnny Cash
2. Ritchie Valens
3. Joe Meek
4. Leonard Chess
5. The Beatles (pre Beatlemania)
6. Bobby Darin
7. Tina Turner
8. The Four Seasons (Frankie Valli and the Four Seasons)
9. Jan and Dean
10. Alan Freed

QUIZ 14 – FATS DOMINO
1. New Orleans
2. Antoine Domino Jr
3. Dave Bartholomew
4. Imperial Records
5. *Lawdy Miss Clawdy*
6. *La-La*
7. 6 (on February 8 1957)
8. *Rock and Rollin' with Fats Domino*
9. *Any Which Way You Can*
10. Hurricane Katrina which devastated New Orleans

QUIZ 15 - HEADLINES
1. Gene Vincent
2. Tommy Steele
3. Little Richard
4. Jim Dale
5. Elvis Presley
6. Marty Wilde
7. Jerry Lee Lewis
8. Buddy Holly, Ritchie Valens and The Big Bopper
9. Eddie Cochran
10. Johnny Kidd

QUIZ 16 – CARL PERKINS
1. Jay and Clay (Clayton)
2. Flip Records (a subsidiary of Sun Records)
3. *Blue Suede Shoes*
4. Perry Como's
5. *Dance Album of Carl Perkins*
6. Johnny Cash
7. *Daddy Sang Bass*
8. *Honey Don't* and *Everybody's Trying To Be My Baby*
9. Derek and the Dominos (Eric Clapton)
10. Paul McCartney

QUIZ 17 – THE RECORD LABELS
1. Imperial Records
2. Decca Records
3. Brunswick Records
4. Atlantic Records
5. HMV (His Master's Voice)
6. Liberty Records
7. Capitol Records
8. Specialty Records
9. Gee Records
10. Mercury Records

QUIZ 18 – BUDDY HOLLY
1. Lubbock, Texas
2. Bob Montgomery
3. Decca Records
4. *Love Me*
5. Norman Petty
6. *The Searchers* with John Wayne
7. The Crickets
8. He isn't wearing his trademark spectacles
9. Maria Elena Santiago
10. *It Doesn't Matter Anymore/Raining In My Heart*

QUIZ 19 – THE SONGWRITERS
1. Jerry Leiber and Mike Stoller
2. Felice and Boudleaux Bryant
3. Lionel Bart
4. Otis Blackwell
5. Eddie Cochran and Jerry Capehart
6. Buddy Holly and Jerry Allison (Norman Petty was also credited but he did not contribute)
7. Melvin Endsley
8. Tommy Boyce and Curtis Lee

9. Vincent Rose, Larry Stock and Al Lewis
10. Roy Orbison and Bill Dees

QUIZ 20 – GENERAL KNOWLEDGE 2
1. *Little Egypt*
2. Tommy Bruce (and the Bruisers)
3. Tom and Jerry (Paul Simon and Art Garfunkel)
4. The Poni-Tails
5. *Come On Let's Go*
6. Atlantic
7. He accidentally shot himself with a pistol
8. *Lipstick, Powder and Paint*
9. Dewey Phillips
10. February 3 1959 (when Buddy Holly, Ritchie Valens and the Big Bopper were all killed)

QUIZ 21 – GENE VINCENT
1. The Blue Caps
2. They were a reference to enlisted sailors in the U.S. Navy, of which Gene had been one.
3. Capitol Records
4. *Woman Love*
5. *Race With The Devil/Gonna Back Up Baby*
6. Cliff Gallup
7. *The Girl Can't Help It*
8. Jack Good
9. Eddie Cochran
10. A ruptured stomach ulcer

QUIZ 22 – WHERE ON EARTH?
1. Downtown, Birmingham (*Promised Land*)
2. New Orleans (*Lewis Boogie*)
3. Kansas City (*Kansas City*)
4. Louisiana (*Polk Salad Annie*)
5. Jackson (*Jackson*)
6. Kentucky (*Kentucky*)
7. California (*California Blue*)
8. Panama City (*Guitar Man*)
9. Greenwood, Missippi (*Greenwood, Mississippi*)
10. Broadway (*On Broadway*)

QUIZ 23 – ANAGRAMS 2
1. *Chantilly Lace*
2. *Maybe Baby*
3. *Telstar*
4. *Stuck On You*
5. *Stand By Me*

6. *Reet Petite*
7. *I Got A Woman*
8. *Breathless*
9. *Honey Don't*
10. *Only The Lonely*

QUIZ 24 - THE EVERLY BROTHERS
1. Don (born February 1 1937, Phil born January 19 1939)
2. Little Donnie and Baby Boy Phil
3. *Bye Bye Love*
4. *Wake Up Little Susie*
5. *Cathy's Clown* (also their biggest ever selling single)
6. *Je t'Appartiens*
7. They enlisted in the United States Marine Corps Reserve
8. On stage at Knott's Berry Farm, California
9. *Brother Jukebox*
10. Royal Albert Hall, London

QUIZ 25 – WHAT'S THE COLOUR?
1. Blue (*A Mess Of Blues*)
2. Green (*Green Door*)
3. Brown (*Charlie Brown*)
4. Yellow (*18 Yellow Roses*)
5. Ebony (*Ebony Eyes*)
6. Orange (*Orange Blossom Special*)
7. Pink (*Pink Pedal Pushers*)
8. Purple (*Purple People Eater*)
9. Red (*Red Sails in the Sunset*)
10. Scarlet (*Scarlet(t) O'Hara*)

QUIZ 26 – THE BRITISH RESPONSE
1. *Donna*
2. *Well I Ask Ya*
3. *Rock With The Caveman*
4. Wee Willie Harris
5. *What Do You Want?*
6. *Jack The Ripper*
7. *A Tribute to Buddy Holly*, it was banned for being too morbid
8. *Don't Knock Upon My Door*
9. *Shakin' All Over*
10. *Livin' Lovin' Doll*

QUIZ 27 – CONNIE FRANCIS
1. Freda Holloway (the film was *Jamboree*)
2. Marvin Rainwater
3. *Who's Sorry Now?*
4. *Stupid Cupid*

5. Jayne Mansfield
6. *Lipstick On Your Collar*
7. *Where The Boys Are*
8. *Connie Sings Italian Favorites*
9. *Vacation*
10. Liberace

QUIZ 28 – GET A JOB!
1. Del Shannon
2. Little Richard
3. Ricky Nelson
4. Jerry Lee Lewis
5. Shakin' Stevens
6. Johnny Cash
7. Lloyd Price
8. Big Joe Turner
9. Billy Fury
10. Chuck Berry

QUIZ 29 – CLIFF RICHARD
1. The Beatles and Elvis
2. India (at Lucknow)
3. The Drifters (then Cliff Richard and the Drifters)
4. *Move It*
5. *Living Doll*
6. Jerry Lee Lewis
7. *Summer Holiday*
8. *Devil Woman*
9. Phil Everly
10. *The Fabulous Rock 'n' Roll Songbook*

QUIZ 30 – GENERAL KNOWLEDGE 3
1. Kay Starr
2. *The Witch Doctor*
3. Vince Taylor (and his Playboys)
4. Roy Taylor
5. Chas Hodges (of Chas and Dave)
6. Drums
7. Huey 'Piano' Smith
8. The Impressions
9. The song was *Let The Good Times Roll* and they were known as Shirley and Lee
10. *Johnny Remember Me*

QUIZ 31 – ALBUM TITLES
1. Fats Domino
2. Jerry Lee Lewis
3. Del Shannon

4. Marty Wilde
5. Everly Brothers
6. Pat Boone
7. Frankie Avalon
8. Chuck Berry
9. Eddie Cochran
10. Jackie Wilson

QUIZ 32 – DUANE EDDY
1. Lee Hazlewood
2. *Rebel Rouser*
3. *Have 'Twangy' Guitar Will Travel*
4. London
5. *Because They're Young* (1960) and *Pepe* (1961)
6. Brenda Lee
7. The Blossoms (as The Rebelettes)
8. *A Thunder of Drums*
9. The Art of Noise
10. A Chet Atkins Gretsch 6120

QUIZ 33 – IT'S A GIRL THING!
1. Marie (*(Marie's The Name Of) His Latest Flame*)
2. Sally (*Long Tall Sally*)
3. Susie (*Wake Up Little Susie*)
4. Lana (*Lana*)
5. Lizzy (*Dizzy Miss Lizzy*)
6. Diana (*Diana*)
7. Fannie Mae (*Fannie Mae*)
8. Sherry (*Sherry*)
9. Peggy Sue (*Peggy Sue Got Married*)
10. Sheila (*Sheila*)

QUIZ 34 – LITTLE RICHARD
1. Macon, Georgia
2. R.C.A. Victor
3. Esquerita
4. *Tutti Frutti*
5. *Slippin' and Slidin'*
6. The Upsetters
7. *Here's Little Richard*
8. Jimi Hendrix
9. *The King Of Rock 'n' Roll*
10. Jon Bon Jovi

QUIZ 35 – IN THE MOVIES
1. *The Girl Can't Help It*
2. *King Creole*

3. *Rock, Rock, Rock!*
4. *High School Confidential*
5. *Go, Johnny, Go!*
6. *Serious Charge*
7. *The Duke Wore Jeans*
8. *Don't Knock The Rock*
9. *Rock Around The Clock*
10. *Play It Cool*

QUIZ 36 – BILLY FURY
1. Liverpool on April 17 1940
2. Larry Parnes
3. *Gonna Type A Letter*
4. *The Sound Of Fury*
5. The Silver Beetles
6. *I Gotta Horse*
7. *Wondrous Place*
8. *Because Of Love*
9. Stormy Tempest
10. Rheumatic Fever

QUIZ 37 – ANAGRAMS 3
1. The Coasters
2. The Drifters
3. The Chantels
4. Bill Haley and His Comets
5. The Flamingos
6. The Crickets
7. The Moonglows
8. The Clovers
9. The Platters
10. The Dominoes

QUIZ 38 – RICKY NELSON
1. Eric Hilliard Nelson
2. New Jersey
3. *The Adventures of Ozzie and Harriet*
4. *I'm Walkin'* on the flip side to *A Teenager's Romance*
5. *Stood Up*
6. James Burton
7. *Hello Mary Lou/Travelin' Man* which reached number 2 on June 7 1961.
8. The Stone Canyon Band
9. *Garden Party*, an 'oldies' concert at Madison Square Garden where Ricky erroneously thought that the crowd were booing him for not performing his old hits.
10. Jerry Lee Lewis

QUIZ 39 – ON THIS DAY
1. Buddy Holly & the Crickets (performing *That'll Be The Day* and *Peggy Sue*) and Sam Cooke (performing *You Send Me*)
2. Elvis Presley, Carl Perkins and Johnny Cash
3. Floyd Cramer with *On The Rebound*
4. Joe Meek
5. Brian Locking
6. Connie Francis
7. Cliff Richard
8. Little Richard
9. Clyde McPhatter
10. Fats Domino

QUIZ 40 – GENERAL KNOWLEDGE 4
1. John Lennon
2. Carl Perkins
3. *What A Crazy World*
4. *Somethin Else* - reached 100 on April 23 1988
5. Nat 'King' Cole
6. Drummer Clem Cattini
7. Twelve
8. Sandra Dee
9. The song was *Secret Agent Man* from *Danger Man*
10. *Not Fade Away*

QUIZ 41 – ROY ORBISON
1. The Teen Kings
2. *Go, Go, Go* (the A side was *Ooby Dooby*)
3. *Roy Orbison at the Rock House*
4. *Claudette*
5. Monument Records
6. *Only The Lonely*
7. *Running Scared*
8. *It's Over*
9. He named himself after his musical hero Lefty Frizzell
10. *Mystery Girl*

QUIZ 42 – NAME THE INSTRUMENT
1. Lead Guitar
2. Piano
3. Saxophone
4. Harmonica
5. Bass
6. Drums
7. Lead Guitar
8. Saxophone

9. Piano
10. Guitar and fiddle

QUIZ 43 – RAY CHARLES
1. Frank Sinatra
2. He had glaucoma from the age of four or five and was blind by the age of seven
3. Nat 'King' Cole
4. Atlantic
5. *It Should Have Been Me*
6. *I've Got A Woman*
7. *What'd I Say*
8. The Raelettes (or Rayletts)
9. *I Can't Stop Loving You* (1962)
10. *The Blues Brothers*

QUIZ 44 – ROCK 'N' ROLL TELEVISION
1. *The Big Beat*
2. Singer Corporation (*Singer Presents Elvis*)
3. *Roy Orbison and Friends: A Black and White Night*
4. Ray Charles and Jerry Lee Lewis (plus Paul Shaffer)
5. Little Darlin's Rock 'n' Roll Palace, Kissimmee, Florida
6. Jerry Lee Lewis'
7. *Rock, Rhythm and Doo Wop*
8. *Blue Suede Shoes: A Rockabilly Session*
9. *Oh Boy!*
10. Howard Hesseman

QUIZ 45 – JERRY LEE LEWIS
1. Killer
2. Ray Price's *Crazy Arms*
3. *Whole Lotta Shakin*
4. *Jamboree* (*Disc Jockey Jamboree*)
5. He was still technically married to his second wife Jane Mitchum at the time
6. *Live at the Star Club*
7. Billy Lee Riley
8. Roy Orbison, Johnny Cash and Carl Perkins
9. *What'd I Say*
10. Rick Bragg

QUIZ 46 – THE SONGWRITERS 2
1. Larry Williams
2. Otis Blackwell and Jack Hammer
3. Artie Singer, John Medora and David White
4. Buddy Knox and Jimmy Bowen
5. Carole King and Gerry Goffin
6. Brian Wilson and Chuck Berry
7. Jerry Leiber and Mike Stoller

8. Doc Pomus and Mort Shuman
9. Roy Orbison and Joe Melson
10. Max Freedman and James Myers (Jimmy DeKnight)

QUIZ 47 – U.K. NUMBER ONES
1. Bobby Darin
2. Frankie Lymon and the Teenagers
3. Tab Hunter
4. Johnnie Ray
5. The Kalin Twins
6. Conway Twitty
7. Tommy Edwards
8. Craig Douglas
9. The Marcels
10. Johnny Tillotson

QUIZ 48 – THE GROUPS
1. The Coasters
2. The Diamonds
3. The Flamingos
4. The Shirelles
5. The Moonglows
6. The Marcels
7. The Drifters
8. The Four Seasons (Frankie Valli and The Four Seasons)
9. The Belmonts
10. The Clovers

QUIZ 49 – SAM PHILLIPS
1. Alabama
2. The Memphis Recording Studio
3. Chess Records
4. Sun Records
5. Marion Keisker
6. It was the first all-female radio station in the United States
7. Jerry Lee Lewis
8. Charlie Rich
9. Shelby Singleton
10. Holiday Inn

QUIZ 50 – GENERAL KNOWLEDGE 5
1. Cliff Richard
2. The Surf Ballroom, Clear Lake, Iowa
3. *Stardust*
4. Ike Turner
5. Carl Perkins
6. Bobby Vee

7. Bill Haley
8. Scotty Moore and Bill Black
9. *Trouble*
10. Roy Orbison

QUIZ 51 – ANAGRAMS 4
1. Ruth Brown
2. Bo Diddley
3. Jerry Lee Lewis
4. Sam Cooke
5. Hank Ballard
6. Johnny Otis
7. Ricky Nelson
8. Little Richard
9. Chuck Berry
10. LaVern Baker

QUIZ 52 – DEL SHANNON
1. Charles Weedon Westover
2. Bigtop Records
3. The musitron (an early synthesiser)
4. *Runaway*
5. *Hats Off To Larry*
6. *Little Town Flirt* (1963)
7. *Ginny in the Mirror*
8. *Keep Searchin' (We'll Follow The Sun)*
9. *The Further Adventures of Charles Westover*
10. A self-inflicted gunshot wound

QUIZ 53 - INSTRUMENTALS
1. The Ventures
2. The Tornados
3. Johnny and Santo
4. Floyd Cramer
5. B. Bumbler and the Stingers
6. Link Wray
7. Booker T and the M.G.s
8. Bill Doggett
9. The Surfaris
10. The Champs

QUIZ 54 – ROCK 'N' ROLL CHRISTMAS
1. *Santa Bring My Baby Back To Me*
2. Billy Hayes and Jay W Johnson
3. *Merry Christmas from Brenda Lee* (1964)
4. Johnny Marks and Marvin Brodie
5. *Merry Christmas Everyone*

6. *A Christmas Gift For You From Phil Spector*
7. Bobby Helms in 1957
8. The Cadillacs
9. The Drifters'
10. *Merry Christmas Baby*

QUIZ 55 – PAT BOONE
1. Dot Records
2. *Ain't That A Shame*
3. *Tutti Frutti*
4. *Long Tall Sally*
5. The El Dorados
6. *Bernardine*
7. Red Foley (writer of *Old Shep* amongst his successes)
8. Bill Haley and His Comets (on *Bill Haley and His Comets*)
9. *Speedy Gonzales* in 1962 (number 6 in the U.S. and number 2 in the U.K.)
10. *Journey to the Center of the Earth*

QUIZ 56 – NAME THE YEAR
1. 1987
2. 1926
3. 1958
4. 1959
5. 1951
6. 1969
7. 1976
8. 1940
9. 1964
10. 1971

QUIZ 57 – WANDA JACKSON
1. *I Gotta Know*
2. *Fujiyama Mama*
3. *Let's Have A Party*
4. *There's A Party Goin' On*
5. *It Doesn't Matter Anymore*
6. *My Baby Left Me*
7. *Two Sides Of Wanda* (1964)
8. Jack White
9. *Funnel Of Love*
10. *Unfinished Business*

QUIZ 58 – NAME THE ANIMAL
1. (Hound) Dog (*Hound Dog*)
2. Robin *(Rockin' Robin)*
3. Alligator (*See You Later Alligator*)
4. Penguins (The)

5. Bird or Dog, or both! (*Bird Dog*)
6. Lion (*The Lion Sleeps Tonight*)
7. Bear (*Running Bear*)
8. Wolf (real name of Howlin' Wolf)
9. Tiger (*Tiger Man*)
10. Monkey (*Too Much Monkey Business*)

QUIZ 59 – WHOSE LINE IS IT?
1. *Here Comes Summer* (Jerry Keller)
2. *Why Do Fools Fall In Love?* (Frankie Lymon and the Teenagers)
3. *Money Honey* (The Drifters)
4. *Fever* (Peggy Lee)
5. *Razzle Dazzle* (Bill Haley)
6. *Pledging My Love* (Johnny Ace)
7. *Splish Splash* (Bobby Darin)
8. *Matchbox* (Carl Perkins)
9. *Blue Monday* (Fats Domino)
10. *Get A Job* (The Silhouettes)

QUIZ 60 – GENERAL KNOWLEDGE 6
1. Elvis Presley, Johnny Cash, Jerry Lee Lewis and Carl Perkins
2. Shelley Fabares
3. Roy Hamilton
4. Johnny Kidd
5. *A White Sport Coat*
6. Roger Peterson
7. *Porky's Revenge*
8. *Roadie*
9. *Little White Bull*
10. Dave Bartram

QUIZ 61 – NEIL SEDAKA
1. Turkey (Ottoman Empire)
2. The Tokens (originally called the Linc-Tones)
3. *The Diary*
4. *I Go Ape*
5. Howard Greenfield
6. *Oh! Carol*
7. *The Same Old Fool*
8. Paul Anka and Sam Cooke
9. *Dream Lover*
10. Jimmy Clanton

QUIZ 62 – ALBUM TITLES 2
1. Sam Cooke
2. Carl Perkins
3. Wanda Jackson

4. Lloyd Price
5. Showaddywaddy
6. Elvis Presley
7. Neil Sedaka
8. Bobby Vee
9. Big Joe Turner
10. Cliff Richard

QUIZ 63 – BRITISH COVER VERSIONS
1. *It's Late*
2. *When*
3. Darts
4. Johnnie Ray
5. Matchbox
6. *Pretend*
7. Status Quo
8. *I Hear You Knocking*
9. *Oh, Boy!*
10. Kim Wilde and Mel Smith

QUIZ 64 – WHO SAID THAT?
1. Bob Dylan
2. Don McLean
3. Elvis Presley
4. Paul McCartney
5. Larry Williams
6. Quincy Jones
7. Sting
8. Little Richard
9. John Lennon
10. Alvin Lee

QUIZ 65 – IT'S A BOY THING!
1. Mack (*Mack The Knife*)
2. Jim (*Jim Dandy*)
3. Jack (*Hit The Road Jack*)
4. Lee (*Stagger Lee*)
5. Willie (*Willie and the Hand Jive*)
6. Gonzales (*Speedy Gonzales*)
7. Larry (*Hats Off To Larry*)
8. Louie (*Louie Louie*)
9. Danny (*Danny*)
10. Johnny (*Johnny B Goode*)

QUIZ 66 – BRENDA LEE
1. 12
2. Little Miss Dynamite

3. *Let's Jump The Broomstick*
4. *Sweet Nothin's*
5. Ray Charles
6. *Rockin' Around The Christmas Tree*
7. *I'm Sorry*
8. *Speak To Me Pretty*
9. The Beatles
10. George Jones

QUIZ 67 – ANAGRAMS 5
1. *Earth Angel*
2. *School Day*
3. *Peggy Sue Got Married*
4. *Little Sister*
5. *Teenage Heaven*
6. *Pledging My Love*
7. *Walking To New Orleans*
8. *Let The Good Times Roll*
9. *I Walk The Line*
10. *Running Scared*

QUIZ 68 – IT'S ALL ABOUT THE NOSTALGIA
1. *American Graffiti*
2. *Back To The Future*
3. *Happy Days*
4. *Quantum Leap*
5. *Forrest Gump*
6. *Dirty Dancing*
7. *Cry-Baby*
8. *Heartbeat*
9. *Hairspray*
10. *Pleasantvville*

QUIZ 69 – ONE HIT WONDERS
1. *Stay*
2. *Mother-in-Law*
3. *To Know Him Is To Love Him* (although one of the Teddy Bears was Phil Spector who of course had many other hits!)
4. *Hey! Baby*
5. *Alley-Oop*
6. *Teen Angel*
7. *Get A Job*
8. *Sea Cruise*
9. *Rockin' Robin*
10. *Lollipop*

QUIZ 70 – GENERAL KNOWLEDGE 7
1. He was stabbed to death by a vagrant on the front steps of his New York home.
2. Johnny Moore (1954–57, 1964–78, 1980, 1983, 1987–98)
3. Jerry Allison (his middle name is Ivan)
4. Frankie Sardo and Dion and the Belmonts
5. *Speedway*
6. Professor Longhair
7. His two eldest sons were killed in a fire at his home in Tennessee.
8. Leonard Chess (he was born in Poland and emigrated to the United States in 1928)
9. Freddie 'Fingers' Lee
10. The '5' Royales

QUIZ 71 – THE SONGWRITERS 3
1. Ronnie Self
2. Berry Gordy, Billy Davis, Gwen Gordy Fuqua
3. Dorsey Burnette
4. Willie Dixon
5. Roy Brown
6. David White
7. Jerry Leiber and Mike Stoller
8. Bernard Weinman and Lee Rosenberg
9. Bobby Charles
10. Credited to Ethel Smith, wife of Bo Diddley – though Bo is accepted to have written it.

QUIZ 72 – THE DRIFTERS
1. Billy Ward and his Dominoes
2. *Money Honey*
3. *Such A Night*
4. *Honey Love*
5. *White Christmas*
6. George Treadwell
7. The Five Crowns
8. *There Goes My Baby*
9. *Kissin' In The Back Row* in 1974
10. Rudy Lewis

QUIZ 73 - GENERAL KNOWLEDGE 8
1. *Grease*
2. Richard O'Brien
3. *Joseph and his Amazing Technicolor Dreamcoat*
4. *Million Dollar Quartet*
5. *Buddy – The Buddy Holly Story*
6. *The Tempest*
7. *Smokey Joe's Cafe*
8. *Are You Lonesome Tonight?*

9. *Baby It's You!*
10. *Dreamboats and Petticoats*

QUIZ 74 – JOHNNY CASH
1. J.R.
2. When he joined the United State Air Force in 1950
3. *Cry! Cry! Cry!* (with *Hey, Porter* on the B side)
4. *Get Rhythm*
5. *Johnny Cash With His Hot And Blue Guitar*
6. The Tennessee Two (Luther Perkins and Marshall Grant)
7. *Ballad Of A Teenage Queen*
8. By saying 'Hello, I'm Johnny Cash'
9. June Carter
10. *A Boy Named Sue*

QUIZ 75 – IN THE MOVIES 2
1. *It's Trad Dad!*
2. *Take Me High*
3. *Change Of Habit*
4. Fabian
5. *Hell Is For Heroes*
6. Shelley Fabares
7. *Be My Guest*
8. *The Fastest Guitar Alive*
9. Johnny Cash
10. *Playgirl Killer*

QUIZ 76 – WHAT'S THE NUMBER?
1. 20 (*Twenty Flight Rock*)
2. 16 (*Only Sixteen*)
3. 1 (*One Night*)
4. 9 (*Riot in Cell Block No. 9*)
5. 60 (*Sixty Minute Man*)
6. 3 (*Three Hours Past Midnight*)
7. 30 (*Thirty Days To Come Back Home*)
8. 16 (*Sixteen Tons* – Elvis only ever sang the song live)
9. 88 (*Rocket 88*)
10. 13 (*Thirteen Women*)

QUIZ 77 – TOMMY STEELE
1. *Singing The Blues*
2. The Steelmen
3. Himself (not Larry Parnes), it was taken from his paternal grandfather's name Stil-Hicks
4. *The Tommy Steele Story*
5. *Knee Deep In The Blues*
6. *Kill Me Tomorrow*

7. Decca
8. *Nairobi*
9. Eleanor Rigby – a bronze statue that he created in 1981 and donated to the people of Liverpool
10. Elvis Presley (with no evidence of it having taken place)

QUIZ 78 – ON THIS DAY 2
1. Alvin Stardust
2. Bobby Darin
3. Larry Williams
4. *Big Girls Don't Cry*
5. The Everly Brothers
6. Elvis Presley
7. Jerry Lee Lewis
8. Capitol Records
9. John Lennon and Paul McCartney's
10. Cliff Gallup

QUIZ 79 – SAM COOKE
1. *You Send Me*
2. Craig Douglas
3. 1986
4. *Chain Gang* in 1960
5. R.C.A.
6. SAR Records
7. *Twistin' The Night Away*
8. The Harlem Square Club, Miami, Florida
9. *Frankie and Johnny* (in 1963)
10. 33

QUIZ 80 – GENERAL KNOWLEDGE 8
1. Ike Turner and the Kings of Rhythm
2. *Let The Good Times Roll*
3. Pat Boone
4. Huey 'Piano' Smith and his Clowns
5. *That Thing You Do*
6. *Weekend*
7. *The Steve Allen Show*
8. The Mann Act – he was convicted of transporting a minor across state lines for allegedly immoral purposes.
9. The Isley Brothers
10. Albert Lee

QUIZ 81 – U.S. NUMBER ONES
1. *The Great Pretender* (February 18 1956)
2. *Heartbreak Hotel* (May 5 1956)
3. *Wake Up Little Susie* (October 21 1957)

4. *You Send Me* (December 9 1957)
5. *At The Hop* (January 6 1958)
6. *Tequila* (March 17 1958)
7. *Yakety Yak* (July 21 1958)
8. *Stagger Lee* (February 9 1959)
9. *Venus* (March 9 1959)
10. *The Twist* (September 19 1960)

QUIZ 82 – BOBBY VEE
1. Robert Thomas Velline
2. He and a group of schoolfriends volunteered to perform in the place of Buddy Holly, Ritchie Valens and The Big Bopper who had been killed that morning en route to the show.
3. *Suzie Baby*
4. Liberty Records
5. Adam Faith
6. *Devil Or Angel*
7. *Rubber Ball* in 1961
8. The Crickets (*Bobby Vee Meets The Crickets*)
9. *What'd I Say*
10. *Take Good Care Of My Baby*

QUIZ 83 – ALBUM FILLERS
1. *Ray Charles*
2. *Rock and Rollin with Fats Domino* (*Ain't That A Shame* was incorrectly labelled as *Ain't It A Shame*)
3. *Rock 'n' Roll Stage Show* (Bill Haley and his Comets)
4. *Summer Holiday* (Cliff Richard and the Shadows)
5. *Trini Lopez At PJ's*
6. *Bluejean Bop* (Gene Vincent)
7. *The Sound Of Fury* (Billy Fury)
8. *Loving You* (Elvis' soundtrack for the film of the same name)
9. *Pat Boone Sings Guess Who?*
10. *Connie Francis Sings Fun Songs For Children*

QUIZ 84 – NAME THE INSTRUMENT 2
1. Drums
2. Double and electric bass
3. Lead guitar
4. Piano
5. Saxophone
6. Lead guitar
7. Saxophone
8. Lead and bass guitar
9. Bass guitar (also rhythm guitar – she played rhythm guitar on Ritchie Valens' *La Bamba*)
10. Drums

QUIZ 85 – THE CRICKETS
1. Buddy Holly, Jerry Allison, Joe B Mauldin and Niki Sullivan
2. *The Chirping Crickets*
3. *Oh, Boy!*
4. *It's So Easy*
5. Earl Sinks
6. Leo Sayer
7. David Box (aged just 21)
8. *In Style With The Crickets*
9. *(They Call Her) La Bamba*
10. Jerry Allison

QUIZ 86 - THE LIVE ALBUMS
1. Bill Haley and His Comets
2. Ritchie Valens
3. Johnny Cash
4. Elvis Presley
5. Sam Cooke
6. Jerry Lee Lewis
7. Wanda Jackson
8. Chuck Berry
9. Ray Charles
10. Ricky Nelson

QUIZ 87 – SONGS THAT INSPIRED THE FILM TITLE
1. *Peggy Sue Got Married*
2. *Stand By Me*
3. *Heartbreak Hotel*
4. *Some Kind Of Wonderful*
5. *Breathless*
6. *Bye Bye Love*
7. *Love Potion No. 9*
8. *Sea Of Love*
9. *That'll Be The Day*
10. *Pretty Woman*

QUIZ 88 – THE WRITERS
1. Peter Guralnick (a biography on Elvis up until he joined the army)
2. Ronnie Spector (her autobiography)
3. B.B. King with David Ritz (his autobiography)
4. Myra Gale Brown (Jerry Lee Lewis' third wife) with Murray M Silver Jr
5. Nik Cohn (an eyewitness account of the 50s and 60s)
6. Philip Norman
7. Ed Ward
8. Ike Turner (his autobiography) with Nigel Cawthorne
9. Bill Haley Jr (the story of his father)
10. J.C. De Ladurantey

QUIZ 89 – SHAKIN' STEVENS
1. Michael Barratt
2. The Sunsets (as Shakin' Stevens and the Sunsets)
3. *A Legend*
4. P.J. Proby
5. *Hot Dog*
6. Rosemary Clooney
7. *Shaky*
8. *Oh, Julie*
9. *Hit Me Baby, One More Time*
10. *Echoes Of Our Times*

QUIZ 90 – GENERAL KNOWLEDGE 9
1. *(You're So Square) Baby I Don't Care*
2. The Nashville Teens
3. The Jordanaires (backing vocalists par excellence)
4. The Hawk
5. Chuck Berry's 60th birthday (the film covered two '60th birthday' concerts from the previous year)
6. *Kansas City*
7. The Chordettes
8. Glen Campbell
9. *Boxtop*
10. *Hernando's Hideaway* by The Johnston Brothers

QUIZ 91 – FIRST LINES 2
1. *Short Fat Fannie* – Larry Williams
2. *Smoke Gets In Your Eyes* – The Platters
3. *Brown Eyed Handsome Man* – Chuck Berry
4. *Not Fade Away* – Buddy Holly
5. *It's Only Make Believe* – Conway Twitty
6. *Stagger Lee* – Curtis Lee
7. *Breathless* – Jerry Lee Lewis
8. *Sea Cruise* – Frankie Ford
9. *Money (that's what I want)* – Barrett Strong
10. *Halleluyah, I Love Her So* – Ray Charles

QUIZ 92 – STARS IN THEIR EYES
1. Gary Busey
2. Tom Hiddleston
3. Dennis Quaid
4. *La Bamba*
5. *It Happened At The World's Fair*
6. *Why Do Fools Fall In Love*
7. Mos Def

8. Little Richard
9. Jamie Foxx
10. Laurence Fishburne

QUIZ 93 – THE STRAY CATS
1. Brian Setzer, Lee Rocker and Slim Jim Phantom
2. *That'll Be The Day* and *Stardust*
3. Dave Edmunds
4. *Runaway Boys*
5. *Stray Cat Strut* (number 3 in the U.S., number 9 in the U.K.)
6. *Built For Speed* (effectively a compilation of their first two U.K. albums)
7. *(She's) Sexy and 17*
8. Britt Ekland
9. Brian Setzer Orchestra – his rock 'n' roll, swing and jump blues project
10. *40*

QUIZ 94 – WHOSE LINE IS IT? 2
1. *Mystery Train* (Elvis Presley)
2. *Pistol Packin' Mama* (Gene Vincent)
3. *Runaround Sue* (Dion and the Belmonts)
4. *Mess Around* (Ray Charles)
5. *Green Door* (Shakin' Stevens)
6. *Under The Moon Of Love* (Curtis Lee)
7. *Mother-In-Law* (Ernie K-Doe)
8. *Riot In Cell Block Number 9* (The Coasters)
9. *Speak To Me Pretty* (Brenda Lee)
10. *Cut Across Shorty* (Eddie Cochran)

QUIZ 95 – 'COVERS' ALBUMS
1. John Lennon
2. Huey Lewis and the News
3. Status Quo
4. The Band
5. Cliff Richard
6. The Beach Boys
7. Chas and Dave
8. Bill Wyman
9. Daniel O'Connell
10. Paul McCartney

QUIZ 96 – THE SONGWRITERS 4
1. Gene Pitney
2. Tommy Durden, Mae Boren Axton (and Elvis Presley got a credit but didn't have any input)
3. Allen 'Dick' Penner and Wade Lee Moore
4. Pearl Lendhurst
5. Henry Mancini

6. Conway Twitty and Jack Nance
7. Felice and Boudleaux Bryant
8. Charles Underwood
9. Robert Blackwell and John Marascalco
10. Jackie Brenston (and Ike Turner who wasn't credited)

QUIZ 97 - SHOWADDYWADDY
1. Leicester
2. Choise and The Golden Hammers
3. *New Faces*
4. Malcolm Allured and Romeo Challenger
5. Dave Bartram
6. *Hey Rock and Roll*
7. *Under The Moon Of Love*
8. *Step Two*
9. *Who Put The Bomp (In The Bompa-a-Bomp-a-Bomp)*
10. Andy Pelos

QUIZ 98 - ELVIS
1. *That's All Right Mama/Blue Moon Of Kentucky*
2. $35,000
3. *I Want You, I Need You, I Love You*
4. *All Shook Up*
5. *Loving You*
6. Col. Tom Parker
7. *G.I. Blues*
8. *Suspicious Minds*
9. 21
10. *It's Now Or Never*

QUIZ 99 – THREE STEPS TO HEAVEN
1. Ricky Nelson
2. Bill Haley
3. Gene Vincent
4. Sam Cooke
5. Chuck Berry
6. Fats Domino
7. Johnny Cash
8. Ray Charles
9. Ike Turner
10. Elvis Presley

QUIZ 100 – IT'S STILL ROCK 'N' ROLL TO ME
1. *The Longest Time*
2. *Crazy Little Thing Called Love*
3. *Crocodile Rock*
4. *Old Time Rock & Roll*

5. Dire Straits
6. *Faith*
7. *Back To Black*
8. *It's Only Rock 'n' Roll (But I Like It)*
9. *I Love Rock 'n' Roll*
10. *Mercy*

FURTHER LISTENING

Through one medium or another, pretty much every rock 'n' roll track ever laid down is available for the interested listener. Here then are some of my favoured rock 'n' roll albums (most referenced in this book) that I feel are best appreciated in their original layout rather than as simply songs within a random compilation.

Back Home (1970) – Chuck Berry
Johnny Cash at San Quentin (1969) – Johnny Cash
Country and Western meets Rhythm and Blues (1965) – Ray Charles
Singin' To My Baby (1957) – Eddie Cochran
One Night Stand! Sam Cooke Live at The Harlem Square Club (1985) – Sam Cooke
The Chirping Crickets (1957) – The Crickets
Getaway with Fats Domino (1965) – Fats Domino
Born Yesterday (1985) – The Everly Brothers
The Sound Of Fury (1960) – Billy Fury
Live at the Star Club, Hamburg (1964) – Jerry Lee Lewis
Roy Orbison at the Rock House (1961) – Roy Orbison
Ol' Blue Suede's Back (1978) – Carl Perkins
King Creole (1958) – Elvis Presley
King of Rock and Roll (1971) – Little Richard
Stray Cats (1981) – Stray Cats
Gene Vincent and the Blue Caps (1957) – Gene Vincent

Printed in Great Britain
by Amazon